Landing Internships and Your First Job

Why Qualifications Are *Not* Enough

Jerome Wong

REAL WORLD

EXPERTS

To my wife, Pauline, for being so supportive throughout the process of my writing this book.

Also to my daughters, Marisa and Kristen, who will hopefully now actually believe what I am saying because it is in print!

Acknowledgments

I WOULD LIKE to thank the great friends who have helped review the various revisions of this book and provided me with invaluable feedback. These friends, listed alphabetically, are Max Chau, Steven Gee, William Ho, Jennifer Jung, Bill Lin, Ravi Nathan, Silvio Proano, Stephan Reckie, Joyce Wong, Daniel Xu, and Steven Zoeller. Stephan deserves an additional shout-out for the seven months of texting at all hours of the night as we obsessed over the book title until it perfectly conveyed my message to students.

Many other friends have shared with me their experiences recruiting college students, provided additional perspectives to complement my own experiences, and exhibited unlimited patience as I bounced ideas off of them. I am thankful for all of their efforts and continued support.

Finally, my parents have always been behind me regardless of whatever endeavor I was pursuing: whether I was changing jobs, moving across the globe in pursuit of my career, or writing this book. They have provided unconditional support for which I am truly grateful.

Contents

Introduction

As more and more students have discovered in recent years, graduating from college no longer guarantees a good job. More people are graduating than ever before, but there are fewer jobs for them to fill due to contractions in the economy and systemic changes in many industries. Meanwhile, skyrocketing tuition costs have led to considerable student debt, making one's first job even more vital for managing debt.

Of course, this is not the first time in their lives that college students have had to compete. Anyone who understands the college admissions process knows that at the competitive universities, there are many more qualified candidates than slots available. That's why, in addition to promoting qualifications such as GPAs, test scores, and extracurricular activities, high school counselors and college admissions consultants emphasize the importance of differentiation strategies like unique achievements, uncommon hobbies, or creative essays to help students stand out from the crowd. High school students who come across as distinctive have a better chance of being noticed, and those who are noticed have a better chance of being admitted to the colleges of their choice.

The same is true once college students begin looking at career options: There are more qualified candidates than slots available for both internship programs and full-time positions. To land the best internship or job, they must incorporate differentiating strategies at every step of the career-prep process to ensure that they stand out and create a strong positive impression on prospective employers.

Unfortunately, the best way to accomplish this is often unclear. The Internet has democratized the flow of information so that anyone can publish his thoughts and opinions—good or bad, correct or incorrect—which leads to a glut of conflicting advice and information that may leave first-time job seekers feeling confused and overwhelmed. How can students discern the good from the bad? The most effective advice would come from someone who knows firsthand what companies and managers are looking for and someone who also has personal experience hiring college students. I meet both of these requirements and gain personal satisfaction from helping student achieve their full potential, which is why I wrote this book. The following pages explain what hiring managers are looking for and thinking about. Using these insights will help you plan the most effective strategies for landing jobs.

I am fortunate to have had exciting and successful careers in both technology and finance. After graduating with a degree in electrical engineering, I worked as an engineer and then in technical sales roles for about a decade. Next, I received my MBA and began my financial career in the emerging area of credit derivatives, the growth of which allowed me to live and work around the world from New York to London to Hong Kong before returning home to the United States.

After twenty-six years in the corporate world, it was the right time for me to do something more entrepreneurial. I had always enjoyed being involved in recruiting efforts, beginning with hiring engineering students as field applications engineers to support my sales efforts in the technology sector and later hiring undergraduate and graduate students into internship, analyst, and associate programs at the banks where I worked. Having conducted hundreds of interviews and having reviewed thousands of resumes over the years, I realized that many college students are not well-prepared for their job searches.

I decided to start my company, Real World Experts™, to advise students on the entire career-prep process. This book shares with first-time job and internship seekers my observations of how recruiting decisions are made in the real world. The strategies, techniques, and anecdotes included in this book are based on my own hiring experiences as well as the experiences of other key decision makers on the recruiting teams I have worked with over the years. Unlike experienced professionals who can point to their relevant work experience as qualifications for future success, students have a more challenging task of convincing prospective employers that their academic and extra-curricular experiences can translate into professional success. They also have the additional burden of convincing companies that they are truly interested and committed to the industry.

The recruiting and interview process is a sales effort where your qualifications, skills, and potential are the services you are marketing. Having spent the majority of my professional career in front of clients as a salesperson and product specialist, I understand the skills needed to convince people to make decisions and take action.

In addition to discussing those skills, in this book I will explain how to:

- Develop creative networking techniques
- Prepare results-oriented resumes
- Engage with interviewers on an emotional level by crafting personal, academic, and professional stories
- Understand the real goal behind many common interview questions
- Provide uncommon answers to common interview questions to have the biggest effect on interviewers
- Create truly insightful questions to shine above the competition
- Demonstrate a sense of urgency and become a low maintenance employee to convert internships into full-time jobs

My objective is to help students effectively communicate their brands and values to potential employers. As you'll see, finding a job is not just about what you've done but about *who you are*, and the advice in this book will help you communicate that clearly, professionally, and in a unique way.

Keep in mind that just as no two candidates are identical, no two interviewers are identical either. What impresses one interviewer may be met with indifference by another, and attitudes and motivations also vary across different industries. The logic and rationale behind the advice I give in this book is explained, as well as potential caveats, so that you will have the framework to decide what works best for you.

I hope you find the information in this book useful and that it gives you the edge over other candidates. I wish you much success and good fortune in your job search and your career.

Chapter 1
Organizational Roles, Functions, and Cultures

MANY INCOMING FRESHMAN do not declare majors because they have not decided what to study and they are even further away from deciding on a career. They often don't need to declare their majors until the end of their sophomore year, which allows them time to explore and discover their interests. During this period of academic self-discovery, students should also take the time to think about career options so that their academic choices complement possible career choices. This chapter provides a framework to explore career options.

Roles vs. Functions

Companies are created to provide a particular product, service, or experience to consumers, other companies, or institutions. Within every company are departments that perform a specific function, such as sales, marketing, manufacturing, finance, or human resources. And within each department are people who perform specific roles that help carry out part of that function. For example, treasurer, accountant, and auditor are all roles within a finance department, and recruiter, benefits coordinator, and development specialist are roles within human resources.

Below is a simple overview that outlines various functions and roles you may find within companies. I've provided it here as a starting point to help you find your ideal role in the working world. The lists and classifications below are by no means exhaustive or definitive, but they should provide a general framework to help you in your search.

Organizational Framework

1. Design and Production Functions and Roles
   - Development and design
     - Scientist
     - Engineer
     - Computer programmer
     - Designer
     - Researcher
   - Operations
     - Manufacturing
     - Plant manager
     - Quality assurance engineer
     - Machinist
     - Technician
     - Finance
     - Treasurer
     - Accountant
     - Financial analyst
     - Logistics

- Distribution manager
- Supply chain analyst
2. Client-Oriented Functions and Roles
   - Sales
     - Salaried vs. commissioned pay structure
     - Inside salesperson (remote client management) vs. outside salesperson (face-to-face meetings)
     - Cold-calling (prospectors) vs. generated leads (closers)
   - Marketing
     - Brand creation/promotion/extension
     - Establishing strategic alliances/third party programs
     - Public relations
     - Advertising
   - Investor relations officer
   - Customer service representative
3. Infrastructure Functions and Roles
   - Human resources
     - Recruiter
     - Benefits administrator
     - Corporate trainer
   - Information technology
     - Database administrator
     - Network administrator
     - Cyber security analyst/engineer
   - Legal
   - Regulatory/Compliance officer
   - Business strategist/analyst
   - Risk management analyst

Finding Your Fit

The degree to which an employee has the right skills, experience, and personality necessary to succeed within a particular role, function, company, or industry—also known as "fit"—has become a popular evaluation criterion for both companies and candidates in recent years. Figuring out fit can be difficult for anyone, but it is particularly challenging for students because they do not yet have the hands-on experience to know what's best for them.

Determining fit is important for two reasons. The first is to ensure the industry, company, and job you choose is a match for your personality, goals, and aspirations. If you choose to start a career that does not align with your priorities and values, you may not last very long in the position. The second is that thinking seriously about fit in advance will help you prepare for interviews. If you have a good sense of where you may fit, you'll be better equipped to answer questions like "Why do you want to work for us?" and "Why should we hire you?"

For example, engineering can encompass a variety of roles, from quality assurance and back-end development to user-experience design. You may have the coding skills required for each, but if you prefer focusing on the highly technical aspects of the function, like computer hacking and reverse engineering, you will probably prefer a back-end development role. If you enjoy thinking about how consumers and clients will interact with the product and you maintain more of an outward focus, you may prefer a front-end design and development role.

This dynamic also applies to sales vs. marketing. People sometimes confuse these terms, and the negative stereotype of the unscrupulous, high-pressure salesman has become so ubiquitous that some may shy away from this particular function out of fear of association. However, doing so might be a mistake if you consider what will be your best career fit.

Salespeople have direct revenue responsibilities for specific clients/territories and are often paid commissions based on the sales they generate. A successful salesperson is a conduit of information between the client and the company. The salesperson's goal is to balance the needs of his clients (best service/product for the best price) with those of the company (maximum revenue). A good salesperson is empathetic, is a good listener, and enjoys interacting with and helping others. There's a common misconception that you have to be extroverted to be effective at sales, but that's not true. Great salespeople have a wide range of personalities, and as long as you enjoy engaging seriously with new people and the art of negotiation, you should consider a career in sales.

Marketing is a step removed from the client. It helps position the products and identify target markets for the company. A marketer works on defining and building the brand, advertising, and creating strategic alliances with other companies to promote her company's brand and products. Marketers also work with customers to determine their needs and price sensitivity and then use that information to help create and promote products. This includes determining the size of potential markets to see whether the products or services are economically feasible for the company to pursue. If you prefer to work at a more strategic level and analyze broad market trends and opportunities, a marketing role may be the right fit.

Infrastructure functions provide the services and support necessary for other areas of the organization to operate efficiently and productively. Increased regulatory oversight such as Dodd-Frank for financial firms and the Clean Air Act for energy and manufacturing companies has contributed to the growth of regulatory and compliance career opportunities. The rise in successful hacking attacks on major government institutions, retail companies, and corporate institutions has elevated the importance of cyber security in information technology departments.

A major advantage of working in infrastructure roles is that because they are support functions, which are less dependent on specific industry expertise, they can offer more latitude to move across industries than other roles like marketing or sales, which generally require more specific product or market sector knowledge. Because the nature of the work is more easily broken down into individual tasks, these roles may also offer more flexibility with regard to flextime and job-sharing arrangements if you expect these issues to be important for you in the future.

Using Values to Determine Fit

In addition to your skills, interests, and personality, you should also consider your values (your core principles and priorities) when determining fit. Understanding your values helps you set goals and find your fit. Some examples of each include:

- Values—loyalty, trust, freedom, security, health, family, happiness, integrity, honesty, stability, fulfill a passion, do good for the world, spirituality, education, free time
- Goals—financial, professional, family, education, travel, spiritual, charitable, fitness, adventures/experiences

When considering which jobs to apply for, take into account whether your values and goals will be aligned with that particular environment and role. First-time job seekers are particularly prone to being enamored by big-name companies and, therefore, may not think through whether the position is right for them. Conflicts between your needs and your work conditions can lead to mixed emotions, anger, and frustration, and prevent you from advancing as quickly as you otherwise would.

For example, while pretty much everyone has financial goals, some people desire stability and just want enough money to live comfortably while others are risk-takers who want to be millionaires. The former probably wouldn't fit into a 100 percent commissions-based sales role, and the latter wouldn't fit into a back office or customer service position. If freedom and work/life balance is important to you, you need to find a position where you can mostly leave work at the office. This would preclude most client-facing roles because you would need to be available to clients on their schedules rather than your own. Better fits would be infrastructure roles such as regulatory/compliance officer or risk-management analyst, which are typically not on call after normal working hours.

Of course, your goals will evolve over time, and that is fine. For example, when I was first starting out, I had a goal to become financially secure. Now, I have set a new one whereby I'd like to have enough money so that I am able to spend more time giving it away than making it. Right now, your goals might be as simple as "earn enough to pay off my student loans within five years" or "become a project leader within two years." If you can identify your goals, you can better assess which jobs will allow you to achieve them.

Corporate Cultures

We have been exploring different roles in organizations and how they may fit with your personality and priorities. Additional considerations include the type of environment an industry or organization offers: the size of the company, the degree of formality, the management hierarchy, and the amount of collaboration encouraged. Process-driven people may find the structure of larger firms more appealing; enterprising people may enjoy the unstructured aspect of smaller firms.

At one end of the spectrum are companies with a more formal, structured hierarchy. This includes most investment banks where the analyst pool waits for work from the associate pools, which waits for work from vice presidents, who wait for directions from their managing directors. At the other end of the spectrum are companies with looser reporting structures and more collaboration. This includes many technology companies, which are project-based and more collaborative (at least within projects). Here, teams coalesce around projects rather than rigid reporting lines. Of course, most organizations have some form of hierarchy and varying degrees of collaboration.

Another aspect of culture involves the work environment—how people actually work and work together. Are the team players or the "lone wolves" rewarded in the organization? Is the office arranged as cubicles, or does it have an open floor plan more conducive to encouraging informal employee interactions? Do employees brag about not taking the vacation time allotted to them? The true definition of "cultural fit" in the corporate world is whether your priorities and preferred work environment are in line with what the company offers.

For example, if you want to work in investment banking or be on the partner track at a law firm, be prepared to work eighty-plus hours per week, including weekends. If you want to be a management consultant, be prepared to live out of your suitcase. You will not succeed in these industries unless you embrace these realities.

Diversity in the work environment may be important to you, either because it provides a support system for you or because you are more comfortable in a less homogenous environment. If you are interested in an organization's diversity, look for signs that can tell you how committed the organization is to creating a diverse environment. Evaluate the company's middle and senior management ranks to determine whether the company is really committed to expanding diversity or just paying lip service to the concept so it may be viewed as politically correct and avoid lawsuits.

I was at a town hall meeting for a company I worked for where the diversity discussion was facilitated by six middle-aged white men; this sent a mixed message to the audience. On the other hand, in the mid-1990s, I was invited to participate in a meeting by human resources because the bank I worked for realized that Asian analysts and associates (such as myself) consistently had the highest turnover rate at the bank, and it was making a sincere effort to find out why. The point is that a company's stated priorities can vary greatly from its actual ones. It may be difficult to know this before actually working somewhere, but you can do research online or ask other people in the industry before you decide to accept a job offer.

LinkedIn and other career and employment websites provide good job descriptions that you can use as starting points to explore what types of roles and environments are a good fit for you. As you meet people at informational interviews, ask some of the following questions so you can better understand whether their roles are a good fit for your personality:

- What do you like best about your role, not necessarily limited to the aspects of the current company?

- What did you find most challenging about your role when you started? Is this challenge a function of your background? Would someone with a different background find it easier?
- How was the job different from your expectations?

The better you are able to determine the best industry, role, and corporate culture fits for you, the more likely you will enjoy what you do and become successful at it.

Chapter 2
The Corporate Recruiting Process

ONCE YOU HAVE an idea what type of job you would like, you need to figure out how to get interviews. Large and small companies recruit at colleges, hiring interns and new grads for entry level positions. However, just because a company doesn't recruit on-campus does not mean it will not hire students and graduates from your school. It just means it will take more persistence on your part to get a foot in the door.

How Do Companies Decide Which Schools to Recruit From?

Not surprisingly, companies recruit at schools with strong academic programs in their fields. Financial services firms flock to the top business programs, while technology companies want the best and brightest from schools like Stanford, UC Berkeley, and MIT. Companies have finite resources, so they also recruit at colleges located close to their headquarters to save on time and travel expenses. Sometimes, legacy issues come into play, with senior managers favoring recruitment efforts that focus on their alma maters.

Most competitive universities cite their prestige and alumni networks as evidence of their students' future job prospects. While it is certainly true that graduates from top schools have access to some of the best jobs, the advantage varies significantly, so students from less competitive schools should not feel disadvantaged or discouraged. Keep in mind that the much greater number of students at large state universities means those schools' alumni networks are larger than those of many smaller, elite, private schools, so make sure you take advantage of all of those contacts if you go to a larger school.

On-Campus Recruiting

The processes and structure for on-campus recruiting for both summer internships and full-time positions are effectively the same. Companies hold corporate information sessions highlighting the virtues of their organizations and then ply students with pigs-in-a-blanket and cocktail shrimp in the networking events that follow.

After that, students submit resumes to secure the much-coveted on-campus interview. Candidates who are selected and go on to ace the interview then proceed to the next battery of interviews in-house at the firm's location. In some cases, the in-house interviews can include up to seven or eight rounds of interviews; sometimes, this last round of interviews is held on a single day known as Super Saturday. After the final interviews have been conducted, successful candidates receive an offer for the internship or full-time position.

Companies use summer internship programs as a feeder program for full-time candidates and, therefore, focus on rising seniors (and some rising juniors) whom they can hire upon graduation. If you're in your first or second year of college and looking to build your resume, but you can't find an internship in your field accepting first- or second-year students, don't worry. You can find other summer jobs where you can develop transferable skills that can help you gain internships in your field in later years. These skills include expertise with spreadsheets, databases, presentation software, and computer programming languages; they are useful for every industry.

Who Makes the Final Hiring Decision?

Some large and midsized companies hire college grads into generalist analyst or trainee programs rather than hiring for specific positions; these new hires are later assigned to specific departments and roles. In this situation, hiring decisions are made by committees rather than by a single hiring manager. Realistically, even in situations where the final decision is made by a single hiring manager, it is very likely candidates will have to interview with several members of the team to ensure a good fit.

In cases where hiring is done by committee, once recruiters finish on-campus interviews, they go back to the office and collectively discuss candidates. This process is analogous to the college admissions process, where admissions committees sit together and review transcripts, standardized test scores, teacher recommendations, and personal essays. Recruiters will compare candidate evaluations to assess qualifications for the position, fit within the group, how professionally and confidently applicants presented themselves, and applicants' knowledge and interest in the company and industry. It is your job to convey your traits to the interviewer through your resume, answers, and the questions you ask interviewers (topics we will cover later in the book). Only then will the interviewer have the ammunition and conviction to be your advocate in these group meetings since decisions are typically not made in a vacuum.

If you listened in on a recruiting meeting, you would hear some version of the following:

- "The candidate was nice enough and seemed smart but nothing stood out, so let's keep looking...."
- "The candidate looked better on paper than in person...."
- "The candidate exhibited a sense of entitlement and didn't know much about the company nor what is happening in the industry...."

To avoid the above pitfalls, it is important to understand what the concerns are behind these statements:

- "The candidate was nice enough...." If the person were hired and became a problem, the hiring manager would lack a good answer if asked, "What were you thinking when you hired this person?" Unfortunately, politics are a part of the real world.

- "The candidate looked better on paper...." The person's writing skills and/or experience were sufficient, but the candidate was unable to tell his story convincingly or present himself in a way that signaled he would be a good fit for the company.

- "The candidate exhibited a sense of entitlement...." The candidate came across as high maintenance, had a poor attitude, and lacked preparation and/or motivation.

Recognizing Corporate Concerns

Companies are concerned about reputational risk and legal liability arising from the actions of their employees. As many job-seekers of all experience levels are aware, companies perform background checks on employees. In the past, companies were limited in how much information they could dig up on potential hires and, unless candidates had criminal records, it was impossible for an employer to know what kind of risk a candidate would be until after the person was hired. Nowadays, the Internet, particularly social media, provides employers a quick and easy way to find out more about a candidate's background. A candidate's judgment regarding what he posts on social media can disqualify him out of concern for the company's reputation, even if he were an otherwise strong contender. In recent years, companies have fired employees for racist or other offensive rants on social media, even though the content did not have anything to do with the company.

Remember, just about anyone can see what you post online, and nothing is ever truly deleted in the digital world, so it's important to think carefully about what you post. I have seen people criticize and complain about the company they work for, their coworkers, and even their own team on social media *from their work locations*. Why would another company hire such people?

Inappropriate attire and offensive language either in person or online are red flags because they reflect poorly on the company with clients or other companies. Demeaning actions against protected classes can create a legal liability for the firm because such actions can create a hostile work environment, and other employees can bring legal action against the firm for allowing or not rectifying conditions. Protected classes are characteristics protected by law, and include (but are not limited to) sex, national origin, race, color, religion, disability, age, and sexual orientation. The intent of the speaker doesn't matter, only how others respond. So even if you're trying to be funny, keep in mind that jeopardizing your career for the sake of a joke is no laughing matter.

Concerns of Hiring Managers

In addition to communicating their own credentials and goals, candidates should also address the interviewer's professional and personal needs. Just like most people, managers want to make their jobs as efficient as possible, promote their own careers, and minimize their risk of hiring poorly-performing employees.

While every interviewer is different, they are all looking for answers to the same basic four questions:

- Is the candidate qualified to do the job?
- Do I want to work with this person day in and day out?
- Will this person fit into my team?
- Does this candidate have the potential to be a superstar?

Your ability to convince the interviewer that the answer is "yes" to all these questions is the key to getting a job offer.

For example, when interviewing for trading positions, some students would tell me they love the markets and investing. One of the questions I would ask was, "If I gave you $1 million today, how would you invest it?" A surprising number of candidates struggled to answer this question, which I interpreted to mean that these candidates liked the trappings or perceived lifestyle of a trader but were not as passionate about trading as they had stated. I have also interviewed economics majors who were unaware of the U.S. debt-to-GDP ratio, the most common metric used to evaluate the indebtedness of countries, particularly after the recent Greek Debt Crisis. This type of glaring disconnect between professed interest in, and actual knowledge of, a sector obviously reflects negatively on the candidates and shows they are probably not a good fit for the company.

Managers need to manage their time efficiently and want to make their own jobs as easy as possible. They look for low-maintenance employees and will avoid potentially high-maintenance employees like the plague. Signs of high maintenance employees are candidates who:

- Complain about being treated unfairly at previous jobs or positions
- Make excuses or blame others for any shortcomings or failings
- Consistently express negativity
- Provide longwinded explanations
- Candidates need to resist the urge to "unload" about prior unfair experiences, regardless of how valid the concerns may have been. The brief cathartic release is not worth the damage it could inflict on your candidacy. Whether the interviewer is a potential manager or potential coworker, neither would want to spend eight to twelve hours a day sitting next to someone who complains all day long.

Another issue is the "manageability" of the candidate. Will the manager be successfully able to manage and motivate this person? Surprisingly (or not), money is not a key motivating factor for many people, so if a manager wants to have a successful relationship with her employees, she needs to make sure she can engage them in other ways. The following aspirations are often more important:

- Purpose—As social creatures, people want to feel their work and opinions matter and they also want to be recognized as valued members of a team.
- Autonomy—People want to be trusted to do

their jobs and need to be given the authority, trust, and responsibility to do so.

• Pride—Employees want to feel a sense of accomplishment and progression in the organization as a metric of success.

When an interviewer asks you what motivates you, you show him you are inherently manageable if you respond based on one of the above factors because these factors are generally within the manager's control.

What Is Human Resources' Role in the Recruiting Process?

HR coordinates the company's school outreach programs, setting up corporate presentations, job fairs, job listings, and on-campus interviews. Depending on the industry and company, HR may have little domain knowledge, or it may be a strategic business partner. It may have varying implicit or explicit hiring power and usually only conduct the initial screening interviews. Its recruiting responsibilities include aggregating and filtering candidates by verifying candidates meet job requirements and possess relevant soft skills, confirming schools/degrees/grades, running background checks, including social media, and verifying work history, if any.

Don't underestimate the role HR plays in the recruiting process because HR employees are the initial gatekeepers and can become vocal advocates if you are able to impress them. Most of the factors they evaluate candidates by are the same as used in other departments, such as a concise, results-oriented resume, knowledge of the company, and professional demeanor and poise. Additionally, HR focuses on something called "Demonstrated Interest." This is the same concept used by colleges to gauge a candidate's interest in attending the school. Did the applicant visit the campus, speak with an admissions officer, or request an interview, if those opportunities were voluntary and available? In career prep, demonstrated interest is your ability to reconcile your stated passion or interest in an industry with the actions you have taken and the efforts you have made in pursuit of a career in your industry of choice. For example, interviewers sometimes ask candidates whether they read trade newspapers or websites. A negative answer is a red flag because it shows that the candidate is not committed to learning about the industry.

During conversations or screening interviews with HR, mention the informational interviews you have had at the company, the corporate events you attended, and even events with other companies you attended to learn more about the industry. Recruiters expect students to engage in a comprehensive job search, so you should not be concerned about appearing uncommitted to one company by mentioning your meetings with other companies. Arrange one or two informational interviews at the company on your own to show initiative, and then ask HR for assistance in arranging additional interviews to engage them in the process. You establish a stronger relationship with HR employees and are more likely to gain their support when they have invested time and effort into developing a relationship with you.

Chapter 3
Planning for Your Career

STUDENTS OFTEN TELL me they are too busy with their coursework to dedicate time to career prep. Unfortunately, attending job fairs or on-campus interviews is not necessarily enough to find a job; you will need to put in a lot more effort if you want to maximize your chances of landing a great first job or internship.

Striking a Balance

People often say that searching for a job *is* a full-time job. For college students, it should at least be a part-time job, which means you should consistently set aside time each week for career prep. Ideally, you should start thinking about career prep efforts as a first-year student, although at this stage, your focus should just be on getting familiar with the career services available on campus, exploring your academic interests, and thinking about establishing academic credentials attractive to potential employers. The term "build your resume" aptly describes the process as it takes many steps over time to create an attractive professional profile.

However, even if you are a junior or senior, you still have many opportunities to stand out from the crowd by presenting your experience and accomplishments in the most attractive manner possible. You also have plenty of time to practice and hone your interview skills and reach out to industry professionals.

Some students view career prep as a seasonal exercise, one they need only prepare for at the beginning of the on-campus recruiting season or when deadlines for summer internships come due. This is a mistake. Just as athletes train during the off-season, students should spend time throughout the year networking, going on informational interviews, and attending industry events to build knowledge and interview skills. If you wait until the end of junior year or the beginning of senior year to think about what to put on your resume, options for gaining more experience or filling gaps become limited.

Perhaps you're worried that if you take time away from studying, your grades will suffer. And wouldn't that affect how you look to a recruiter or potential boss? The answer is—not really. Let's assume that the marginal difference between a 3.62 and a 3.70 GPA is irrelevant to the vast majority of employers. Over the first three years of college, that is approximately the difference between receiving an A and an A- in six classes, which equates to one class per semester (as-suming a total of twenty-seven classes over the three-year period).

How much time per week would you have spent earning the additional 0.08 increase in your GPA? Thirty minutes? An hour? What additional career opportunities would you have created for yourself if you invested that time, across the span of three years, into career development instead? The point is not that academics aren't important, because they are. Rather, it's that every decision has tradeoffs, and students should be aware of the opportunity costs of their decisions. This numerical example should provide some food for thought for students looking to manage their time in school most effectively.

Experienced professionals are equally guilty of not striking a good balance. Understandably, family and job pressures and priorities override the need to manage their careers through networking and keeping abreast of industry and job trends. Many people only actively start exploring options after layoffs are announced at their companies, which makes them appear desperate—because they probably are and it will show. As you progress in your career, an important adage to follow is, *"It is easier to find a job when you have a job."*

Academic Planning

You have a much better chance of establishing optimal academic credentials when you start planning early. As you consider selecting a major, or if you have already chosen one, also think about the complementary skills you want to develop to build the most attractive academic credentials. The professional and academic worlds have become much more multi- and cross-disciplinary, so you need to select majors, minors, and coursework strategically. Universities offer many exciting cross-disciplinary majors, such as behavioral economics, computational neuroscience, biophysics, computational sciences, and data science, all of which meld together previously independent disciplines, thus allowing you easily to broaden your expertise. In addition to positions in these exact fields, these degrees also afford you the opportunity to be considered for a broader range of career choices.

Even if these programs are unavailable to you, or not in line with your interests, you can always craft your own academic plan to suit your needs. For instance, if you are majoring in engineering, you can balance your technical skills with a minor in business or marketing; such a minor will allow you the option of pursuing management, technical, or sales tracks if you decide that's in line with your goals or you can't find a suitable job in engineering. If you are an art history major, consider a minor in accounting or computer science. That way, if you can't find a curator position, you can find a position in another department, such as finance or marketing in a museum or art gallery, giving you the chance to work your way through an organization to your desired position. Two or three courses are all you need to gain proficiency and the skills needed for entry-level work if you don't want to declare a minor in such a field.

Taking classes or minoring in entrepreneurship is not just useful for starting a business, but it is also great career prep because it gives you a broad overview of the different functions necessary for almost any business to operate successfully. After all, the skills needed to convince investors to buy into your startup are a lot like those needed to convince upper management to fund a project you are proposing. Think of entrepreneurship programs as mini-MBA boot-camps, exposing students to issues faced by all organizations—from start-ups to conglomerates, and from for-profits to non-profits.

Research positions, where students assist professors with their projects, are great ways to differentiate yourself and provide many opportunities to show-case your thought processes and initiative. Think about the questions below and how you may use the answers in an interview:

- How did you find the position? Did you take any particular initiative to get the role?
- What other areas were you considering, and why did you finally choose this topic?
- What skills have you gained from the experience?
- What results were expected/unexpected?
- What are the next steps in the research project? (Even if you're no longer working on the project, you can provide context for its long-term goals.)
- How has this experience affected your career direction?

Independent study courses are even more differentiating than research projects because they require more initiative in proposing a topic and following through mostly on your own, as opposed to working under a professor's specific direction. Choose a topic that has broad applications so it will be of interest to as many potential employers as possible.

For instance, Big Data—the use of large datasets and quantitative information to make decisions—is a current area offering many research opportunities in a wide range of fields. For example, in medicine, big data is now being used, thanks to advances in technology, to help diagnose concussions—a process that is still mostly qualitative and inexact. Technology has been developed that incorporates accelerometers (which exist in every smartphone for detecting motion) into football helmets to measure the impact of collisions that result in concussions. The goal is to create a large database so that in the future when an impact occurs, the characteristics of the impact are immediately checked against the database to determine the likelihood and severity of a concussion.

Data analytics for retail and e-commerce is another area where big data has exploded: Companies track user preferences based on the websites they visit, the things they post or "like" on social media, whom they follow on social media, past purchasing patterns, and a slew of other information to predict retail trends and target consumers. The U.S. economy has consistently been driven by the consumer (approximately 70 percent of gross domestic product), so data analytics is an important area of growth.

The Internet of Things is another area that is growing exponentially. An example of an industrial application of this emerging field would be a large power plant using remote sensors to, through the Internet, measure the performance and condition of machine parts, alerting techs before failures, rather than waiting for the machinery to break down or performing unnecessary maintenance based on a schedule. Performing necessary maintenance based on objective, quantifiable data can save time, money, and resources.

Another example is using sensors inside buildings to monitor central air conditioning vents for airflow and temperature at every vent to optimize and save energy, rather than relying on room thermostats, which only sample the temperature of a single, localized area.

The common theme for these examples is: Through the collection of a large amount of data, more informed decisions can be made. In addition to the technology sector, the opportunities to apply this methodology to medicine, healthcare, retail, and the social sciences are limitless.

While building an academic profile to maximize your knowledge and skills is important, it's not the only thing to consider when choosing what to study. Your time in college should also be an opportunity to challenge yourself intellectually, discover new passions, and explore subjects outside of your comfort zone. It would be a real shame if you didn't expand your horizons and have some fun with courses outside of your academic requirements. Not only is this part of the college experience, but it may also help you in interviews. After all, if the person conducting the interview is going to have to work with you eight-plus hours a day, she is going to want you to be interesting and well-rounded. Plus, having a unique story to tell the interviewer about an unconventional class or experience will help you stand out, which is always important.

Industry and Company Research Framework

You can make a strong, positive impression on your interviewer by showing a practitioner's understanding of the company and industry. This information would be useful when the interviewer asks you what you know about the company or why you want to work for it. Use the following framework to help research companies, understand their business, and see how changes in the industry affect them:

- What are the strengths and weaknesses of the company with respect to product and service offerings, geographic client coverage (local, regional, national, or global), and client demographics (by age, sex, race, income)?

- How is the competitive environment? Is the number of competitors entering the space increasing or is the industry consolidating? Is a change in demographics driving this change?

- Are there significant barriers to entry, such as high capital costs or intellectual property issues (pharmaceutical under patent)? Is the company competing with brands that have become synonymous with their product categories, such as Scotch® tape, Frisbee®, Jacuzzi®, Styrofoam™, Jell-O®, and Band-Aid®?

- What are possible substitutes? For example, smartphones have crowded out tablets and laptops. Streaming music and video have up-ended CD and DVD markets. Fast food, fast casual, and full-service restaurants all have to compete for the same dining dollars.
- What are potential disruptive technologies?
- What regulatory and environmental issues and challenges does the company face?

To find the answers to the questions above, you can use a variety of resources:

- Company websites and annual reports
- Company press releases
- RSS feeds
- Industry news from newspapers, industry publications (The Internet is a vast source of data; the challenge is to filter and gain useful information.)
- Networking contacts
- Informational interviews

Research reports from brokerage companies are another source of industry and company information. You can open a discount brokerage account with a small investment and then gain access to the firm's research. This information is provided so clients can make investment decisions; you can use this same information to prepare for interviews.

Using Your School's Career Services Office

You are already paying for career services as part of your tuition, so you should definitely take advantage of the facilities. Resources will vary from school to school, but every school will provide at least some job search assistance, which can include coordinating on-campus corporate recruiting, organizing job fairs, posting jobs from companies that don't recruit on campus, posting notices for informational interviews from alumni, and preparing resume books (binders of resumes sent by Career Services to prospective employers).

Career service offices also offer training services, such as resume reviews and cover letter assistance, which help students prepare for their job searches. One of the most useful services they provide is mock interviews, where the student's performance is videotaped and then reviewed with a career advisor. These sessions can be very revealing because students are often surprised by how they appear on video; everything from their posture and ability to maintain eye contact, to the number of times they say "like" or "um" is there to see on screen.

Case study interviews are popular with management consulting firms. If you are interested in this field, find out whether your career services office offers sample questions, frameworks to analyze different categories of questions, and specific interview practice for case studies.

Career advisors can also provide personality tests, such as the Myers-Briggs Type Indicator*, to help students discover the industries and positions that best match their goals and personalities. The results can introduce you to industries or roles you may not have previously considered.

As mentioned earlier, the Internet can provide potentially conflicting career advice, so you should take advantage of access to career advisors for additional insight into career topics you are unsure how to address. Ask the advisors to explain their viewpoints so you can judge for yourself. Career services personnel have a vested interest in helping students find jobs because successful students reflect well on the school and their department.

Chapter 4
Building Your Personal Brand

JUST AS COMPANIES establish brands to differentiate products and services, you can also develop your own personal brand to help communicate who you are and help you stand out from the competition. Your personal brand will be important throughout your career and especially useful when applying for jobs. While some companies—especially highly technical companies—will value skills more than personality, all interviewers will consider your personality to some degree, consciously or not, when assessing you for a position.

When it comes to career planning, your personal brand is comprised of the two or three personality traits or skills you want your interviewer to remember. I suggest two or three because any more than that would be difficult for the interviewer to remember and support with any conviction. In the thirty or forty-five minutes of the typical on-campus interview, it is challenging, if not impossible, for interviewers to discern these traits or skills unless you proactively spell them out. Prepare your answers to interview questions by providing several examples to reveal each trait or skill. We will go into detail on exactly how to do this in Chapter 10.

As you think about the image you want to establish, consider the perspectives and concerns of potential employers. Doing so will help you preempt and dispel negative stereotypes and highlight attributes that companies value. In any sales situation, identifying and addressing the needs and requirements of your client is key to closing a transaction successfully. The same is also true when you are interviewing for jobs; understanding the issues that hiring managers face will help you create a compelling story about why you would be a great hire.

Addressing Generational Stereotypes

Upon entering the workforce, many young adults are thrust into an environment where they will have to interact with Baby Boomers, Generation Xers, and other Millennials. Language, priorities, and perspectives are unique to each individual, but they are more similar within generations than across them. These differences affect how people communicate and interact, as well as how they perceive people from other generations. These issues matter because Millennials who are looking for entry-level jobs today often have to confront the stereotypes and preconceptions of their interviewer, who will likely come from an older generation.

Unfortunately for new job seekers, Baby Boomers and Gen Xers often assume that Millennials are self-centered, entitled, and self-indulgent—not attractive traits for a potential hire. These characteristics reflect a poor attitude and manifest themselves in different ways, such as resting on academic laurels, believing that certain tasks are "beneath" them, and having unrealistic career progression expectations.

A Human Resources recruiter called a young candidate to schedule an interview. The student responded that he was in the middle of having lunch and that he would have to call back. This true story, though atypical, reinforces the stereotype that the current generation is self-centered. If you are not in the middle of something urgent, stop what you are doing and take the call because you don't want to take the risk that the HR representative fills up all the available interview slots before you've had a chance to call him back.

In another situation, a candidate was on hold with an airline trying to book a flight home in the midst of a family emergency. When a recruiter called to schedule an interview, the candidate said she would have to call back but didn't provide an explanation as to why. Despite having a valid reason for not being able to talk at the moment, the candidate lost the opportunity because the recruiter followed up with another candidate instead of waiting for the first one to call back. It is impossible to know whether this person would have gotten the job if she'd behaved differently, but in my experience, recruiters are willing to be accommodating if candidates fully explain their circumstances and provide specific plans to follow up.

Regardless of whether you agree or disagree with these perceptions of Millennials (or the next generation), they exist, and it is up to you to prove them wrong. Some of these issues can be addressed on your resume by highlighting experiences that showcase your diligence and willingness to work hard. For example, I once reviewed the resume of a college student in his senior year and noticed that he only listed a single internship. He explained that he had previously listed his summer jobs working for a landscaping company but was told by an advisor at his school's career services office that he should remove them because they were not directly relevant to his major.

The advisor may have had the best intentions, but the advice offered was outdated by several decades. With previous generations, employers were much less concerned, if at all, about whether a candidate had a sense of entitlement. However, it is a common talking point among interviewers now. I suggested that the student keep his summer positions on his resume and, in the description, state that he'd worked in landscaping to help pay for his tuition. By having these positions on his resume, the student demonstrated that he was not afraid of hard work and immediately dispelled any concern that he felt entitled.

Showing Your Demonstrated Interest

Companies are interested in what students do in pursuit of their career interests and the initiatives they take in addition to using the broadly available resources on campus. Therefore, you should reach out to industry professionals in as many different venues as possible to gain some practical knowledge of the industry. Reaching out can include scheduling informational interviews, becoming involved with industry associations, and attending Meetups.

You can join the school newspaper to create access to senior industry professionals as a reporter. You can write a blog with your thoughts on your industry; you can even just be a curator and list interesting articles from other sites with some color commentary. These activities support your interest in the industry and can be useful to include in cover letters and thank you notes.

Attitude

Curiosity and an open mind led to groundbreaking but accidental inventions like penicillin, the microwave oven, and dynamite. These qualities are also among the most highly-valued personality traits in the working world. Many managers, including myself, list a positive and can-do attitude as one of the more desirable characteristics we look for in candidates. This encompasses an unquenchable desire to learn, intellectual curiosity, and a sense of urgency. In today's world of constant change, employers are looking for people who can adapt and thrive in an unpredictable environment.

When interviewing, you can demonstrate your positive attitude as part of your brand when answering personality questions such as, "What are your key strengths?" or "What was the biggest obstacle or challenge you overcame?" The strategies for answering personality questions will be explained further in Chapter 10.

Our structuring group at a large bank spent a lot of time creating spreadsheets to model cash flows under many scenarios—which required a lot of computing time. A young analyst took it upon himself to code up the models in VisualBasic because he saw the spreadsheet models ran too slowly. He wasn't asked to do this and he didn't ask for permission; he just did it and we were all very pleasantly surprised with the outcome. He was smart and hardworking, but he was also taking initiative—a fact that was just as, if not, more important than his skills or knowledge. He subsequently became a managing director by the age of thirty.

As discussed earlier, stereotypes about Millennials need to be addressed. One of the main concerns is a sense of entitlement.

An analyst confided in me that after working three months in our group, she wasn't learning anything at all and was being treated like a secretary. She had graduated from a top school and felt she was being marginalized. The conversation went as follows:

Me: What do they have you doing?

Her: All I am doing is putting together PowerPoint presentations. That's it.

Me: You are in a marketing function. That's what you should be doing.

Her: But I'm not learning anything.

Me: Show me the last presentation you put together.

(She retrieved the presentation, and I pointed to the transaction diagram.)

Me: Explain to me why the client would want to enter into this transaction.

Her: Uh, I don't really know.

Me: Explain to me how our bank makes money from this transaction.

Her: Uh, I don't really know that either.

Me: So, the lessons were right in front of you, but because you treated it as a secretarial task, that's exactly what you got out of it.

In the above example, if the analyst had approached any of the more experienced team members, we would have been happy to explain the transaction to her. The moral of the story here is that you get out of tasks what you put into them.

On another occasion, an associate at a bank had come to me for advice on how to speak to his manager about getting an early promotion. I was open to helping him and the conversation went as follows:

Me: How would you evaluate your work and accomplishments over the past two years?

Him: I did everything my manger asked me to do.

Me: What did you do above and beyond what your manager had tasked you with?

Him: Well, I accomplished everything on time, and

> when I asked how I was doing, my manager said fine.

Me: So the answer to my question about what you did above and beyond is nothing?

Him: Uh, I guess nothing, really.

Me: By definition, you are competent because you were successfully able to complete the tasks assigned to you. Great. Now you are asking for an exception to the promotion schedule, but you can't support the request with any exceptional work or accomplishments. Do you see the disconnect here?

Him: I do see what you mean. Thank you.

This employee subsequently asked his manager for an early promotion and, not surprisingly, was denied.

It is not only Americans of the Millennial generation facing the entitlement issue; China's one-child policy has been in effect long enough that current students are now known as the 4-2-1 generation; four grandparents and two parents doting over one child. The one-child policy has led to a generation of "princelings," which evokes images of spoiled, self-indulgent young adults. Again, perception can trump reality, so it is important to preempt negative stereotypes.

Self-Confidence

Self-confidence is one of the top traits hiring managers cite as a reason they find candidates attractive. People tend to trust those they view as confident, so it is important to be able to convey this characteristic to hiring managers. Confidence is communicated by the content of your statements, but even more importantly, by your tone and demeanor when delivering that content.

One of the biggest ways both first-time job seekers and seasoned professionals inadvertently demonstrate a lack of self-confidence is by hedging their comments and suggestions by saying things like, "I could be wrong, but…" or "I'm not sure, but…." Or they deliver statements with a rising inflection, as if they were asking questions rather than supporting an idea or viewpoint, needing someone else to validate their contribution.

Hedging your answers in interviews in either manner is a bad idea (even when done unconsciously, which it typically is) because it is a total lose-lose strategy. Even if your answer is correct or your idea is good, you won't receive much credit for it because you made it obvious that you were unsure. So why do so many people do this? My theory is that people don't want to be associated with wrong answers, so they try to appear non-committal. When you answer confidently, you will position yourself to get credit for being right. When you don't, you are negotiating against yourself, and that will show up as a lack of confidence.

During interviews, anxiety levels increase and students will appear less confident in the face of uncertainty. This especially happens when they feel they have not prepared sufficiently for the interview. The solution is simple: Make the effort to prepare as thoroughly as you can, and you will naturally feel more assured going in.

Professionalism

Many of the aspects of professionalism come under the heading of common sense; however, as one of my favorite sayings goes, "*Common sense is not common.*"

Professionalism includes:

- Dressing appropriately
- Showing up early or at least on time
- Treating others with respect, especially subordinates
- Paying attention to details
- Completing tasks on time
- Not making excuses
- Not complaining or saying something is not your job
- Accepting constructive criticism graciously
- Not being a drain on your manager's time
- Avoiding inappropriate language or humor

Dressing appropriately, being punctual, and being respectful are actions that can be exhibited during the interview process. Enthusiastically greet the receptionist and thank the employee who brings you to the interview room.

A person's lack of attention to detail is difficult for an interviewer to determine from an interview, though it may be revealed by typos in a cover letter or resume. Failure to pay attention to details is a difficult issue to correct, and it is the quickest way to lose credibility with your manager. Unfortunately, I have had to let people go because of their lack of attention to detail, despite a strong work ethic and raw intelligence. In a business where a small mistake can easily cost millions of dollars, I really have no choice when it becomes a pattern. It is difficult to demonstrate a strong attention to detail during an interview; however, it can be an important characteristic for you to point out when asked by interviewers how former managers or associates would describe you. This is one of the only situations in which you can work this important trait into a conversation.

Chapter 5
Creative Networking and Job Search Techniques

N OW THAT WE'VE covered how to establish your qualifications and reviewed the traits necessary to make you attractive to potential employers, it's time to turn our attention to the actual job search process. This involves figuring out all of the resources at your disposal to contact prospective employers.

Networking is an integral part of the job search process, allowing you to learn about the industry and identify available positions. One of the most effective ways to network is through social media, especially LinkedIn. LinkedIn is becoming more popular with students as they realize it is a vital resource used by professionals. Once you set up a profile, connect with everyone you possibly can: friends, relatives, relatives of friends, current professors, former teachers, and alumni from all of the schools you have attended. When you meet people at corporate presentations or informational interviews—anywhere someone gives you a business card—invite them to connect on

LinkedIn. Some professionals will accept the invitation and some will not because they are more guarded with their network, but it definitely doesn't hurt to ask.

Your LinkedIn profile is an important platform to reinforce your brand but also to show your personal side. Put a face to the name and personalize your profile with your picture. Since it is likely that an interviewer has already reviewed your resume before viewing your profile online, do not simply repeat the information from your resume in your profile. The tone of your LinkedIn profile should be more conversational, so convert some of the bullet points on your resume to prose to provide additional context. For example, your resume may include a bullet point such as, "Increased club membership 20 percent by creating additional social media marketing efforts, including WeChat and other sites foreign students use more often than Facebook." Your LinkedIn profile may read, "We increased club membership 20 percent by reaching out to foreign students on WeChat and other social media platforms used outside the United States. This led to increased diversity and a club-organized trip to visit companies in China over the winter break."

If a recruiter or potential employer is looking at your LinkedIn profile, that means you have already passed the first filter because the academic and extracurricular successes on your resume have convinced that person to find out more about you. Build upon your resume by posting examples of your portfolio if you are in a creative field or examples of websites and games you have created if you have any comput-er skills. Also, list any industry conferences or events you attended.

LinkedIn is a combination of formal and social con-tent, and the information you provide should reflect this balance. Add pictures showing academic or club activities to augment the activities mentioned in your resume. Think about including your "bucket list" or fa-vorite books to show your personality. Make your sto-ries sound interesting. For example, don't just list scuba-diving as an interest—add color by explaining that you received your diving certification in Phuket, Thailand, and your goal is to dive the Great Barrier Reef.

Adopting a Sales Mindset

Sales and marketing professionals know that appeal-ing to emotions and promoting experiences often helps drive consumer decisions—often even more ef-fectively than a rational analysis of product features and benefits. Interviewers, although they might not realize it, operate in the same way, making hiring de-cisions based on their emotions, rather than strictly focusing on candidate qualifications. Applying sales perspectives and techniques to the job search process will help you engage interviewers on an emotional level, where you can more easily convince them to hire you from among a pool of other well-qualified candidates.

Being an effective salesperson requires influencing others to take an action (ideally, in favor of the sales-person). The best salespeople "show, not tell," so cus-tomers feel they have come to their own conclusions, which is much more powerful than being told what to think or do. Some students may be uncomfortable "tooting their own horns," and others may not know how to do it well without sounding conceited or arrogant. Telling an interviewer how smart or how hardworking you are does not effectively convey any information; all you have done is made a claim without any supporting evidence. A more effective strategy is to let your story highlight your traits. Describe your academic, extracurricular, and work experiences, and let them speak for you. Instead of saying you're a hard worker, explain that you spend ten to fifteen hours a week working at your part-time job, while carrying a full course load during the school year. Instead of saying you take initiative and you are a problem solver, describe the time you led your fellow interns in an effort to revamp a database application at your company.

Approach networking opportunities such as informational interviews, corporate presentations, and job fairs as sales opportunities. The strategies used will vary depending on the event. For example, you should be less aggressive and talk less in informational interviews since the purpose of these is to gain information, not to convince someone to hire you. On the other hand, at corporate presentations or job fairs, which are explicit forums for self-promotion, you can and should draw more attention to yourself. However, you can use informational interviews as an opportunity for some self-promotion because it's likely the interviewer will ask questions about your interests and background.

Sales can be difficult for many people because the fear of rejection can be overwhelming, so people will naturally try to avoid such situations. Even if you do not choose to pursue a career in sales, you have to engage in some selling of yourself, which might be uncomfortable because, up until now, you've likely been in a position where you were able to let your actions speak for themselves. Your teachers, coaches, etc. had to pay attention to you, and if you performed well, you were rewarded accordingly. But now, your past performance is not sufficient; you need to be able to convince recruiters that such performance is indicative of the value you bring to the company. CEOs often come from the sales and marketing divisions of companies because they have the experience and perspective required to lead businesses, so if you are interested in moving up the corporate ladder, work on improving your sales skills.

In addition to adopting a self-promoting attitude and developing the necessary communications and rapport-building skills, adopting a sales mindset requires that you learn how to manage time and plan ahead. Sales is a numbers game, and success depends on continually filling your pipeline with prospective clients. You will increase your chances of landing a job if you similarly invest the time and effort throughout your college career in developing a strong, broad network of contacts in your target industry.

Constructing Your Elevator Pitch

The concept of an elevator pitch initially applied to entrepreneurs, but it has since been adapted for job seekers. If you only had thirty seconds to speak with a recruiter or hiring manager, what would you say to convince her to call you in for an interview? If you take the time to craft an elevator pitch, you will be prepared to engage new people quickly at networking and recruiting events when you are asked, "Tell me about yourself," or "What are you interested in doing?"

First, follow the typical guidelines for establishing an engaging conversation. Smile to show self-confidence and put people at ease. You will be viewed as more friendly and will, therefore, set a more open tone for the conversation. Mention a common acquaintance (if available) at the beginning to establish rapport/ commonality. It is also important to listen and not dominate the conversation.

Next, explain what created your passion in the position or industry, rather than focusing on your relatively limited experience; your passionate tone will then have an emotional effect on the person you are speaking with. As a student, even with some industry experience through internships, it is more important to explain why you are interested in the job or industry. If you have the time, talk about specific things you've accomplished at previous jobs/internships. What did you find particularly interesting?

Finally, close the conversation with a request for a meeting to explore opportunities at the firm or a specific position if there is an internship or program you are aware of. If the person is very senior, it may make more sense to ask for a contact person who is directly involved in the recruiting process whom you can follow up with.

Here's an example of good content for an elevator pitch: "I really got hooked on computer science after completing a project that reproduced Google Earth. The thought that I had the ability to create a program that could be used by millions of people was a bit mind-blowing. By the end of the class, I had gained the confidence that I would be able to tackle any project assigned to me."

This example succinctly related a well-known product to the student's personal development. The initial reaction of being overwhelmed by the project's enormity was genuine for a first-year student without much programming experience, but that reaction then turned into confidence as the semester progressed. It is important to show how the experience materially affected her decision to choose her major.

Reaching Out to Industry Professionals

Contacting alumni from your high school or college is a tried and true method for meeting professionals in your industry. School alumni associations, LinkedIn, and Facebook are all good sources for locating alumni. Sending email is the most efficient way to contact alumni—you may have to reach out a few times, but I find that people are typically open to helping students as long as they are courteous and respectful. You can increase your chances of a response if you establish rapport by doing some research and mentioning a recent announcement or accomplishment of the alumnus in your email.

For various business reasons, I have sent emails to Fortune 500 CEOs, a Nobel Prize winner, senior managers, and other professionals and have received some positive responses for my efforts. Some were fellow alumni from high school or college and others were not. Not everyone responds, but some do, so it is worth making the effort to reach out. Do not feel intimidated by the titles of potential contacts. Perhaps surprisingly, senior people are often more responsive and willing to help than those in entry-level positions. It's possible they want to "pay it forward" by helping students get a start in the business.

Your professors can be good sources for professional contacts since some are industry veterans and others continue to be consultants for companies in their fields. Many will have former students who may also be good contacts for you. I have known students who have gained positions through their professors, so it is definitely worth checking with them.

Meetups are great opportunities to get to know professionals in your target industry. Events can be found at www.meetup.com. Sessions are available for every possible interest: technology, finance, media, marketing, healthcare, sciences, and more. You can even find targeted groups such as Women in Finance, Blacks in Technology, and Women in Product. Industry-specific meetups are good opportunities to network while simultaneously learning about trends in your field of interest.

Consider joining industry trade associations like the Institute of Electrical and Electronic Engineers (for electrical engineers) or the American Marketing Association (if you're interested in marketing). Members receive the association's periodicals and access to industry events, and many have student membership rates that are substantially less expensive than the normal rates. Reach out to the authors or people who are mentioned in the articles to see whether you can schedule an informational interview with them. The same goes for presenters at industry conferences; even if you can't attend the conference, the agenda is usually available online. It is not too hard to figure out someone's corporate email address if it is not listed since most companies follow the same template for all email addresses. If email isn't an option, try reaching out on social media or go about it the old-fashioned way, calling the company directly and asking to be put through.

Many companies understand that diversity is important because teams consisting of members with diverse backgrounds and life experiences can draw on a richer set of viewpoints and perspectives than homogenous groups. To promote diversity, these companies establish and promote employee affinity networks for women, veterans, African-Americans, Hispanics, Asians, people with disabilities, as well as those from the LGBTQ community or certain religious affiliations. These are similar to clubs you find on college campuses, where people with common interests share their experiences and provide support for each other. If any of these affiliations apply to you, reach out to human resources employees at your target companies and ask them to connect you with members of the network. These employees are motivated to promote diversity because it is an important issue for them and can also help advance their own careers. For these reasons, they can become vocal advocates for your candidacy if and when you apply for a job.

In addition to company-specific diversity initiatives, industry-wide organizations, such as the National Center for Women & Information Technology (NCWIT), work with companies to promote diversity in hiring decisions. Other examples include the National Venture Capital Association (NVCA) Diversity Task Force and the Structured Finance Industry Group's Women in Securitization initiative. Reach out to them and their members for advice as well as potential employment opportunities.

A student interested in an internship in the music industry found her college career center listed few opportunities in that sector. To relieve her disappointment, she fell back on the tried and true strategy of retail therapy and purchased a CD by her favorite artist (this was before online streaming). She looked at the back of the packaging, saw that the recording company was located in town, and then called it directly to see whether it offered internships. The company replied that it was thinking about starting an internship program and asked whether she would be interested in coming in for an interview. Over the next dozen years, the student rose from intern to a senior management position at that same company.

If you cannot establish any type of connection

through your existing network, you have absolutely nothing to lose by cold-calling people to see whether they will give you some of their time. At the very least, you have demonstrated initiative, which may be the catalyst to create an opportunity for yourself.

I have given interviews to candidates who cold-called me and even ended up hiring one. The student I hired attended a school that did not have a recruiting relationship with Wall Street firms, so he arranged his own interviews. He had to plan several months ahead because he was from a different part of the country and conducted all of his interviews over his spring break. This showed initiative—he did not solely rely on the resources available to him from the college's career services department but chose to create his own destiny.

Informational Interviews

Informational interviews are useful because they allow you to learn about an industry and see whether it is a field you want to pursue. *Do not* try to convert an informational interview into a job search conversation by asking whether the company is hiring. That will damage the tone of the meeting. Anyone who agrees to give you an informational interview knows exactly why you are there, but she agreed to an informational interview only. If she knows of any opportunities that would be a good fit for you, she will bring it up without you having to ask. In that case, you should be prepared to meet with additional people in a more formal context during the same visit, so make sure you prepare and dress accordingly.

Informational interviews are good opportunities to ask questions that can help you prepare for formal interviews. For example, "What disruptive technologies/trends/forces are on the horizon that will be damaging to the industry or create opportunities for the company?" The answer to this question can be used as the basis for preparing your own questions for a future interview: "I understand that brokerage companies are using technology to reach Millennial clients to lower costs, but that this target demographic is not accustomed to paying for services without first seeing the value of the services. How does your company plan to make money under this new client paradigm?"

Gain contacts for additional informational interviews and maintain the relationships to establish your network. Nurture the relationships by checking in with your contacts from time to time. Ask for their thoughts about events in the industry or background for interviews you have either within or outside their organization.

Corporate Events and Job Fairs

Staffing at corporate events both on- and off-campus include recent alumni, company hiring managers, and human resource representatives. Since many students attend these events, they can often feel competitive, with students trying to outdo one another in order to make the most memorable impression on the professionals in front of them.

These encounters are analogous to the first sales call with a new client, during which less-experienced salespeople will erroneously attempt to oversell the client on the company's product or service. Experienced salespeople know that the singular goal of a first sales call is simply to secure a second sales call, period. The same goes for corporate job fairs and events—don't be overly aggressive in these situations. When speaking with corporate representatives, be sincere and respectful of their team as well as other students. Don't oversell yourself. Simply ask whether you can follow up with them at a later time and collect their business cards or email addresses.

A common mistake students make in such situations is approaching a representative, asking what department he works in, and moving on if the answer is not of interest to them. You never know how this person might be connected to the people you want to meet or how much influence he has within the company at large. Any contact is potentially a great contact, so make the effort to engage in a meaningful conversation with the people you meet even if they may not be from the specific department you are interested in.

Online Resources

Organizations often list employment opportunities, including internships, on their websites or other online platforms. The best places to find relevant job listings are:

- Company websites
- Industry association/trade group websites (Financial Industry Regulatory, American Bankers Association, Institute of Electrical and Electronics Engineers, American Mar-

keting Association, etc.)

- Government websites (Federal Reserve, U.S. Securities Exchange Commission, World Bank, International Monetary Fund, Centers for Disease Control, National Institutes of Health, Food and Drug Administration, NASA, Jet Propulsion Laboratory, Lawrence Livermore National Laboratory, MIT Lincoln Laboratory, U.S. Department of Energy, etc.)

- Internship/job websites (University Career Action Network [UCAN], www.wayup.com, www.linkedin.com, www.internships.com, www.internweb.com, www.monster.com, www.indeed.com/internships, and www.the-muse.com)

As mentioned previously, professional websites such as LinkedIn and the others listed above are a great resource because they allow you to search for internships and drill down based on industry, company, location, and keywords, such as major or field of interest. However, regardless of how you find a job posting, don't just start blindly applying. Instead, reach out to any contacts you have at the company. Failing that, engage friends and family to go through their LinkedIn contacts and alumni networks to help find relevant contacts within the target companies. A good contact can give you additional information about the job, the name of the hiring manager, and make sure your application gets in front of the right people.

If you're reaching out to someone for the first time, be straightforward and tell that person how you found his name and contact information. Ask about the person's experiences with the company and, after you get a response, say you are interested in a position you read about. Ask whether the person would be okay with you mentioning your conversation when you apply for the position. Hiring managers are more receptive to applications that come from people with existing connections to the company, so having someone to mention is a big plus. Depending on how your interaction goes, your new contact may even offer to pass your resume along personally, though you should not presume he will.

Chapter 6
Results-Oriented Resumes

RESUMES ANSWER THE "what" questions all employers have: What have you accomplished in previous positions (professional or otherwise)? What skills have you developed? What have you achieved academically and within your community? In later chapters, we'll discuss how to address the "How" and "Why" questions in interviews and cover letters, but a stellar resume is the first step in getting your application noticed.

An inverse relationship exists between the number of words on your resume and the amount of time a recruiter will spend reading it. Resumes create a first impression on the reader before a single word is read, and dense, block paragraphs are an immediate turn-off. This situation is especially true when recruiters are reviewing many resumes at one sitting, such as when they go through resume books from schools. Your resume's purpose is to get an interview, not to explain every aspect of your life story. Successful interviews are what will get you the job offers.

Make Your Resume Stand Out

This advice is common and pragmatic, but most sources don't provide practical steps on *how* to craft a great resume to get interviews. Advising job seekers to make their resume "stand out" without any further guidance is like a financial advisor telling you the secret to getting rich is just to "buy low and sell high" and then leaving you to figure out for yourself when you actually should buy and sell.

The first question students should think about is not what they can write on their resumes to stand out but rather what they *did* to stand out, which they can then highlight on their resumes. Which activities or roles have you participated in that are unusual given your background? Did you start a business that had employees or was particularly profitable? Did you create an internship or research role for yourself where none existed? These are powerful examples of demonstrating initiative.

Volunteering at hospitals or nursing homes, tutoring in underprivileged neighborhoods, and participating in sports are worthwhile but commonplace activities. Traveling overseas to less-developed countries to help villages build water pumps or volunteering at foreign schools and orphanages are less common because of the expenses involved, but they are also not uncommon. Include these activities on your resume to demonstrate you are well-rounded and because they may create talking points with some interviewers. However, you can tell a more compelling story if you can show that you *affected some change* in these programs rather than just participated in them. For example, did you help recruit additional volunteers, design or introduce new services for a program, or expand existing ones? The point is to demonstrate how you went above and beyond what was required and expected.

Interviewers are impressed by the actions you have taken in pursuit of your interests beyond what you have done in school. Mention any courses you may have taken on Khan Academy, Code Academy, or any other online educational organization to demonstrate your intellectual curiosity and initiative.

What have you accomplished that was not typically expected from your position or was particularly impressive given your level of experience? For example, on my own resume, I highlight the fact that I created an advisory business and participated on an IPO team, two things that are common for investment bankers but highly unusual for those like me who worked in a financial markets capacity and typically only get involved with trading functions.

Format

Organize your resume so the most important points are easy to spot and all of the content is balanced and easy to read. The most common format is a reverse chronological listing of positions, with sections including Education, Professional Experience, Honors and Awards, and Extracurricular Activities. Another well-known format is a skill-based layout that replaces the list of position descriptions with descriptions of skills. For example, technical resumes would list skill categories such as software packages, programming languages, and project management tools, while more generalist, non-technical resumes would list skill categories such as communications, management, sales, marketing, or organizational skills.

Additional rules for formatting include:

- Use traditional 10-point fonts or larger
- Balance use of white space with at least ¾" margins
- Use bullet points, avoid paragraphs
- Keep formatting and alignment consistent for dates, capitalization, abbreviations, bullet point styles, etc.
- Avoid the overuse of bold, italics, and underlining because too many formatting transitions can be distracting
- Do not use unnecessary/obscure abbreviations
- Keep it to a single page (unless you have published many research papers)

Content

Use a professional-sounding email address because your resume is a business document and is often the first contact you have with a company. You want to present a professional image and avoid a negative first impression with an odd or immature email address. It should include your first and last name so email recipients can immediately recognize the email is from you.

Some resume formats include a career objective in which the applicant explains what type of job/role he is looking for. Advocates say that stating career objectives allows employers to get a quick, clear sense of how the applicant is positioning him- or herself, but I am not a fan of this format for a few reasons. For one, these objectives focus the resume on what the applicant wants, not what the applicant can do for the company. Resumes should be about communicating how you can be an asset to the company, not the other way around. You are also disqualifying yourself from consideration for other possible positions because you have already "staked out" what you want to do (the situation is different for experienced professionals or career changers).

Each item on your resume should fulfill a specific purpose:

- Demonstrate a product or industry competency
- Explain a process competency or progression
- Highlight an achievement or result, qualitative or quantitative
- Create a talking point for interviews

Use active verbs to show the results achieved in each item; otherwise, there is no purpose in listing the item. Use verbs that highlight your skills and your brand. These include:

- Analytical: analyzed, calculated, determined, evaluated, solved, studied
- Communication/people skills: addressed, convinced, drafted, explained, negotiated
- Leadership: chaired, coached, directed, initiated, managed, motivated, supervised

- Teamwork: assisted, collaborated, encouraged, facilitated, organized
- Technical: assembled, calculated, computed, designed, programmed

Qualitative results can include taking an action or inspiring a change in behavior or process. For example, your research helped the company decide to enter a new geographic or demographic market or resulted in improved customer satisfaction. Quantitative results can include financial improvements in revenue or costs/time savings, an increase in the number of clients, or a higher click-through rate (a measure of advertising effectiveness) for digital advertisements.

Students have told me it is difficult for them to show direct results of their efforts because they were only working on a small part of a much larger project. If the project achieved impressive results, it is fine to mention your contribution in the context of the overall project. For example, "Analyzed customer demographics which determined that the energy beverage company was missing the largest growth market, leading to a new marketing campaign targeting college students."

You can use information about the company from before you joined it if it adds to your story. For example, I worked for a company that had helped find the *Titanic* a few years before I joined, but the equipment was still a part of the company's product line during my tenure. Later, when applying for a different job, I used this colorful historical fact to add intrigue to my resume by mentioning, "The company's products were used to help find the wreck of the *R.M.S. Titanic*." A similar strategy can be used for any developments that occur after you leave a position. Maintain contact with former groups so you are aware of results and successes that may be useful to incorporate in your resume.

The most common mistake candidates make on resumes is listing day-to-day tasks in a given position rather than what their efforts accomplished for the company, clients, or their manager. Examples of this mistake include:

- "Worked with a senior financial services representative reviewing client cases."
- "Provided fundamental and technical analysis for portfolio manager."
- "Researched consumer preferences for online food delivery services."
- "Supported marketing manager to expand strategic relationships."

None of the above statements contain any results or accomplishments; they just explain what the candidate worked on during the day. If your work experience looks like a posted job description, it isn't a good resume. Your job here is to focus on results, not responsibilities.

The second most common mistake is not providing sufficient detail. The following examples are getting a step closer to effective content but are still not quite there:

- "Maintained the corporate website to facilitate interactions with clients."

- "Contributed to conferences and events to improve brand awareness."
- "Developed marketing campaigns to generate new business and support the sales teams."

The problem with these statements is that they leave the reader hanging because they fail to answer obvious questions:

- "Maintained the corporate website to facilitate interactions with clients."—How much did interactions increase after you took over? This is an easy metric to measure with Google analytics or some other similar service.
- "Contributed to conferences and events to improve brand awareness." Was there an increase in foot traffic at the company's booth and requests for marketing materials at conferences? Did more people sign up for future events?
- "Developed marketing campaigns to generate new business and support the sales teams." How much did sales increase?

These examples show cause and effect, the results of the work done:

- "Provided analysis that showed decreasing gross margins of company X, which led the Portfolio Manager to sell his equity positions in the company across several portfolios."
- "Developed marketing campaigns on Twitter, Instagram, and Facebook to generate new business, resulting in a 35 percent increase in advertisement responses."

- "Automated the MySQL customer database to create more targeted sales campaigns, decreasing marketing costs by 25 percent while maintaining customer response levels."
- "Increased club membership by 20 percent by expanding social media marketing efforts to include WeChat and other sites that foreign students use more often than Facebook."

A common question students ask is whether they should include their grades on their resume. Definitely list your GPA if it is strong—3.5 or higher on a 4.0 scale (or 3.3 or higher for technical fields such as computer science or engineering). If your GPA for your major is higher than your cumulative GPA, list it separately. Alternatively, if there was a dramatic improvement over time, separate out your GPA for the last two years because that may show a recruiter that you have matured and "gotten your act together." A strong GPA indicates that you have the fortitude for future success, even if you are applying for a position that has little to do with your major.

Don't list your GPA if it is lower than a 3.0 since it will likely be viewed negatively. If your GPA is between 3.0 and 3.49, use your judgment when deciding whether or not to list it. You will not necessarily be rejected if you don't list your GPA, but the person reading your resume may wonder what you're hiding. A missing GPA just means the rest of your resume will have to "work" a little harder to get you an interview.

Do not list coursework that is required for your major unless you are a first or second year student without much experience or extracurricular activities and truly need some resume filler. List exceptional classes, such as a graduate-level course or coursework that highlights marketable skills outside of your major. For example, if you are a comparative literature major and took marketing, finance, or any computer-related courses, definitely list these courses under your education section.

Part-time jobs at fast-food restaurants, construction, or any other retail or manual labor positions all help to establish a student's personal brand and dispel any concerns about entitlement. They might not be directly relevant to the job for which you're applying, but they show that you are willing to work. Keep the description short since not a lot of explanation is necessary for these types of positions, but be sure to include any accolades you received in these positions—a promotion, raise, or any other formal recognition. There is no need to list all such positions; your most recent one is sufficient to make your point.

There is no reason to state that you answered phones, confirmed appointments, or filed documents, unless you are looking for a position answering phones, confirming appointments, or filing documents. It's assumed that if the phone rings, you are willing and capable of answering it. Instead, present even your more mundane experiences in the most attractive light possible to communicate your brand. For example, if you were a receptionist at a doctor's office, your job description could look like this:

- Answered patients' questions regarding new

patient forms, insurance coverage, and payments (people skills).

- Coordinated pre-authorizations with insurance companies to ensure procedures were covered (people skills).
- Supported the office manager with scheduling, billing, and vendor communications (team player).

Include your high school only if it is at least regionally well-known. Otherwise, the only reason to identify your high school is if you accomplished something exceptional while you were there that you want to highlight, such as an academic distinction or athletic achievement.

Only list language skills if you are fluent or if they're directly related to the job. Otherwise, you run the risk of being tested on something that doesn't actually matter to your qualifications—and you may be asked to conduct the entire interview in Portuguese.

List hobbies and other extracurricular activities where you can illustrate consistency, a leadership role, or a championship. Err on the side of caution by omitting interests that may be controversial (for example, involvement with the NRA or Planned Parenthood) unless you are specifically targeting an organization where such interests are advantageous (a conservative think tank or women's advocacy group, for example).

Finally, it goes without saying that your "references are available upon request," so there's no need to waste valuable resume space by saying so.

Technical Skills

Employers do not expect interns or new graduates to be subject-matter experts on day one. They will provide on-the-job-training to new employees, and some organizations will also provide formal training programs. Companies understand that there will generally be a transition period for newly-minted college graduates to learn differences between what they were taught in school and how business is actually conducted. During this transition, it's possible, though unlikely, that, as an economics major, you may be asked for your views on GDP growth, or that, if you are a marketing major, you will be asked for ideas for a new product. The more typical tasks for interns or new graduates are to provide operational leverage to the team, which means they will support or expand upon the work of the group's more senior members. These tasks include, but are not limited to:

- Research
- Collating data
- Formatting data
- Automation of manual processes (such as incorporating spreadsheet calculations directly into documents or reports)
- Processing data and information for clients or internal use

To perform the above tasks and show you can provide immediate value to potential employers, students should be well-versed in as many relevant applications as possible. Examples include:

- Presentation software

- Spreadsheets
- Databases
- Statistical packages or language
- Photoshop or Adobe Illustrator for designers
- Google Analytics or other web analytics packages for e-commerce professionals
- Matlab, R, or some other high-level technical computing language and interactive environment for research or technical positions
- Computer programming language(s)

Incorporate technical skills into your work experience content rather than listing them in a separate "computer/technical skills" section. This provides context for the skills and shows how they were used in real-life situations. An exception may be if you are a computer science major or software engineer, where you may want employers to see the breadth of your technical abilities in one place. Otherwise, examples include:

- Used Google Analytics to determine that a new marketing initiative had increased the website's click-through rate by 20 percent.
- Prepared PowerPoint presentation for a new cosmetics brand proposal to senior management, targeting the high-growth Millennial market.
- Analyzed the correlation between oil and natural gas prices using R to create a hedging strategy for a large energy company.

With the exception of people who work in the technology industry, current students are generally expected to be more computer literate than previous generations since they have grown up more immersed in technology. When I was creating a presentation for a website, most of my friends over forty had no idea what Prezi was (a dynamic and visual presentation application), whereas the people I spoke with who were under twenty-five were much more aware of the platform (which is used in many TED talks). Technology you view as commonplace may not be familiar to someone who is a bit older. Therefore, make sure you include your competency with the latest software packages on your resume, even if the project it was used for was not particularly outstanding since the point is to highlight a product competency.

Quality Control

Do not provide reviewers with an excuse to reject your resume. Some of them will throw out a resume and reject the candidate for a single typo or grammatical mistake. This might sound harsh since everyone makes mistakes, but, on the other hand, how can a manager trust a candidate who cannot properly proofread her own work on such an important document? Such mistakes bring into doubt the candidate's attention to detail, particularly when a manager is reviewing a number of other resumes that do not have any typos.

Therefore, before you send off your resume even after minor edits, always make sure to check it for spelling and grammatical errors. Are your subjects and verbs in agreement? Are there any misplaced or incorrect modifiers? Do not rely on grammar checking software to catch these mistakes because they often fail to recognize common errors and may even introduce new ones. Spell-check software will often not catch misused but correctly spelled words, such as "principle-protected investment" vs. the correct "principal-protected investment."

Make sure you've used consistent fonts, formats (bullets, dates, abbreviations), and alignment. You can review in show paragraph marks mode to check for formatting inconsistencies. Always send your resume as a PDF to ensure the formatting doesn't change on another computer.

It always helps to have a few people proofread your resume before you send it along. This will help you spot errors and also get feedback on the content in general. Is it clear and concise? Does it make you stand out?

Don't lie on your resume. This sounds obvious, but it happens more often than people think. With today's computer background checks, it is almost impossible to lie and not get caught.

A colleague mentioned in his resume that he graduated from college when, in fact, he had completed all of the coursework but never officially graduated. He was immediately terminated once the company found this out.

Finally, keep in mind the purpose of the resume—to get an interview, not to get an offer. I once advised a candidate who already had a positive screening interview with human resources. He wanted the recruiter to focus on certain parts of his resume in discussions with the hiring manager. However, the resume had already served its purpose. Instead, I told the candidate to tell the recruiter which talking points he most wanted to highlight rather than continuing to rely on his resume.

Chapter 7
Compelling Cover Letters

THE PURPOSE OF a cover letter is to explain the "whys" of your decisions and engage the reader on an emotional level by explaining how and why you got interested in the field. The most common mistake candidates make in cover letters is to repeat the accomplishments already covered in the resume. Don't miss the opportunity to provide a larger context for information in your resume and explain how your skills and qualifications are relevant to the job you are applying for.

Take into consideration your audience; for instance, a cover letter sent to a line manager might benefit from more details on your technical experience than one sent to an HR representative. Therefore, even if you do not customize your resume for each position, you do need to personalize your cover letter. If the reader senses you sent a form letter, he will quickly toss it into the vertical file (a.k.a. the wastebasket) because you have demonstrated that you are not really interested in the position.

A cover letter should be no longer than one page with a maximum of three or four single-spaced paragraphs. If it's any longer than that, the reader will rush through it or bypass it altogether because it requires too much effort from someone who likely has dozens, if not hundreds, of other letters to read. Less is more, and the important points will stand out if there is less clutter.

If you are responding to a job posting or cold-calling a company, find out who will be evaluating your candidacy so you can properly address that person. Either call the human resources department or send an email to ask for the person who will be reviewing your information. If you are unable to get a response, address your cover letter with "Dear Hiring Manager." Do not use, "To Whom It May Concern," because it sounds impersonal and outdated.

The purpose of the cover letter's first paragraph is to introduce yourself to the hiring manager. It should include:

- A mention of the most relevant acquaintance(s) you have with the company. People are more likely to continue to read a cover letter if they recognize a familiar name early in the letter. This could include current or former employees, a client, friends, family members, alumni from your college, or a representative you met at an informational interview, on-campus presentation, or industry event. If you cannot reference an acquaintance, explain how you were able to find the hiring manager.

- The position or department for which you are applying.
- A brief explanation of your specific academic or professional experiences that qualify you for the role. Don't oversell yourself at this point since this is still part of the introduction.

The second paragraph is the main body of the cover letter and should explain the "whys" and the "hows" behind the information in your resume. These will also help reinforce your personal brand. What do you want the company to know about you? What qualities do you have that should make it want to hire you? Choose the one or two points below that are most relevant to your own experiences, and add a third paragraph if it is needed to complete the details of your story.

- What hardships or circumstances (socioeconomic or personal) did you overcome to achieve your professional or academic success? (tenacity, perseverance)
- What networking methods did you use to gain prior positions? (initiative, creativity)
- Who or what influenced your interest in the company or industry, and why were you so impressed? (motivation)
- Did you teach yourself spreadsheets, a programming language, or some other software package to accomplish a result in your resume? (motivated self-starter)
- Did you write for the school newspaper or have your own blog? If yes, point out a link to an

article you wrote and weave it into your story.

- What activities did you engage in that may not be appropriate for the resume but could provide a memorable anecdote or highlight a trait, skill, or perception of you?

Cover letters should have a more conversational tone than resumes, so they provide a perfect way for you to explain experiences listed on your resume that may benefit from additional context.

A telecommunications manager for a large corporation was called upon to assist at the command and control center during the 9/11 attacks in New York City. This might not fit easily in his resume since it was temporary and not an official position, but it allows the candidate to highlight the fact that his peers consider him an expert in his field. Such an experience could be mentioned in his cover letter, creating a story to engage the reader by explaining who contacted him and what his responsibilities were in such highly unusual circumstances.

A more fitting story for students may be how someone affected their lives or perspectives. For example, a friend recounted the story of how the most respected person in her high school was the janitor. He did his job with tremendous pride and always had time to share practical advice with students. The lesson she continues to remember is that if you always strive to do your best regardless of what you do, you can have a positive effect on people's lives.

Though at first some students may find it strange to include this type of story in a cover letter, one of the cover letter's goals is to explain who you are through an authentic story. It is also a unique and differentiating narrative to convey your brand.

Remember, the requested qualifications on a job posting are the company's wish list rather than absolute requirements—even the the academic major specified. Lead with and focus on your strengths because employers hire you for what you can do. Do not negotiate against yourself. This may sound obvious, but some applicants try to explain a deficiency in a qualification mentioned in the job description. Even if you are lacking a skill the employer is asking for, there is no need to highlight that in the cover letter. You can convince the employer at the interview that your other skills and strengths outweigh a single deficiency. If the job is very attractive to you, start to develop the skill before the interview and bring that up in the interview. Highlighting the issue in the cover letter provides an easy reason to reject your application.

Close the cover letter with a follow-up plan, but do not be presumptuous by asking to schedule an interview. For example, "I would love to meet with you to discuss any opportunities you feel I may be a fit for. When would be a convenient time for you?" Though this may not sound very aggressive, it can be viewed as such because you are committing the recipient, despite leaving the details of the meeting open. There are exceptions to every rule; you may want to be aggressive if you are going for a sales position and want to demonstrate your proactive attitude.

In most cases, I suggest you ask whether you can schedule an interview or a phone call to discuss the specific position or to explore opportunities for which the employer feels you may be suited. For example, "I would love to discuss any opportunities you feel I may be a fit for and would appreciate it if we could have a phone conversation or meeting. Thank you in advance for your time and consideration."

While the content of your cover letter is key, the way you present it could make or break your chances of being asked for an interview. Writing is a key communications skill, so you want to ensure a strong, positive impression by avoiding:

- Weak openings or limiting phrases: "I hope/think/feel…."
- Extraneous phrases: "It goes without saying…," "My viewpoint is…," or "The reason is that…."
- Self-serving statements: "I am the perfect/most qualified/best candidate." Your resume should demonstrate why you are qualified without you having to say it.
- Redundant terms: final outcome, foreign import, plan ahead, etc.
- Grammatical mistakes and typos!

Finally, because the cover letter is a form of professional correspondence, always address the recipient as Mr. or Ms., not by his or her first name, and close with a formal letter closing such as "Sincerely" or "Kind Regards."

Chapter 8
Conversation Skills for Interviews

I WILL SAY it again: In situations where hiring decisions are made by committee, it is your responsibility to provide your interviewers with the ammunition they need to advocate for your candidacy. You need to start preparing to best convey your brand long before you sit down for the interview so you will stand out from all of the other qualified candidates.

Interview preparation consists of ensuring your appearance establishes a positive first impression. It also includes studying current news and trends in your industry and the company to demonstrate your interest in the field. Developing effective communications and interpersonal skills are a must for optimal interview performance. Preparing creative answers to common interview questions and insightful questions to ask interviewers are the keys to differentiating yourself from other candidates.

Non-Verbal Skills

An oft-cited statistic is that 70 percent of communication is non-verbal. Regardless of the exact percentage, you can communicate a lot of information without saying a word, and interviewers (as well as people in general) form an opinion of someone within seconds based on:

- Appearance: Are you neat and well-groomed or unkempt and slovenly?
- Posture: Are you upright and alert or slouching?
- Attitude: Are you confident? Shy? Arrogant?

You really do only have one chance to make a first impression, so make sure you appear open and confident so you can start off on a positive note. Make sure your clothes are freshly pressed, and check your appearance in front of a mirror before leaving for interviews. Does your hair need to be combed? Is there food in your teeth? Also, check that your breath is fresh. Even if you're interviewing for a job in a casual industry, like tech, where the dress code is less professional, you should always opt to wear business clothing. You will never make a bad impression by being *over*-dressed.

If you're a man, get a haircut if necessary. Be clean-shaven or make sure your regular facial hair is groomed. Your shoes and belt should match, and your shoes should be shined. If you are wearing a tie, it should just cover the top of the belt buckle, and shirt sleeves should be slightly longer than jacket sleeves. If you're a woman, avoid heavy makeup, flashy jewelry, over-powering perfume, and overly revealing clothing. Skirts, if worn, should fall below the knee, shoes should be closed-toed, and your hair should be neat. If you're wearing nail polish, make sure it's fresh and not chipping.

An international student met a banker at a corporate event on campus. The banker was impressed with him, but the student ended up accepting a job at a different institution. Within a year, a reorganization put his job at risk and he reached out to the banker for advice because he was concerned about his visa status. The student showed up to their meeting wearing flip-flops; the banker was surprised that the student did not feel it was necessary to maintain a professional appearance because it was not a social meeting and, therefore, the banker was not comfortable sharing his contacts with this student.

While interviewing a Ph.D. candidate, I kept glancing under the table until he asked me what I was looking at. I told him that wearing white tube socks with a dark suit was an unusual fashion choice. He responded that he didn't have time to find dark socks since he had just arrived in New York from Boston late the previous evening. He could have easily found a twenty-four-hour drugstore. Except in extreme circumstances, there are really no excuses for not being well-groomed at an interview or any other professional meeting.

You can also use non-verbal techniques to help build rapport with your interviewer. These include:

- Smiling to exhibit confidence and openness.
- Tilting your head slightly to show trust when

listening to the interviewer.

- Occasionally leaning in slightly to show interest when the interviewer is speaking.
- Squaring your shoulders and hips to the interviewer to demonstrate openness.
- Avoiding defensive postures like folding your arms and crossing your legs.
- Maintaining consistent eye contact—without staring. A common complaint about interview candidates is their inability to maintain eye contact. It is distracting for the interviewer, and it makes the candidate seem evasive or insincere. If maintaining eye contact makes you uncomfortable, look at the interviewer's eyebrows instead and she will still think you are maintaining eye contact.

Listening skills are an important part of establishing rapport, but listening is not the same as hearing. Hearing is merely the physical act of receiving acoustic signals. Active listening is about being attentive and focusing on the speaker to absorb the information he is conveying. Resist the urge to interrupt in order to show how smart you are or to finish the other person's sentences—both of these habits are rude and disrespectful.

Verbal Skills

Taking a page out of the sales handbook, your goal is to engage the interviewer (as a salesperson does with a client) on an emotional level and to address her concerns. What does the interviewer need or want, and how can you make her understand that you can provide it?

As discussed in the introduction, interviewers make hiring decisions based on emotions rather than just a strictly rational analysis of candidate qualifications. Skills and accomplishments convince the interviewer that you are qualified to do the job, but explaining your motivations, aspirations, and values (answering the "why" behind your decisions) will help evoke emotions such as empathy and trust from interviewers. If the interviewer can relate and connect with you, it increases your chances of receiving a job offer. You can also trigger the interviewer's emotions by portraying positive personality traits like sincerity, open-mindedness, confidence, eloquence, and listening skills.

Candidates should not wait to be asked questions during an interview; instead, they should engage with the interviewer in an interactive dialogue. Creating a dialogue involves answering and asking questions that elicit additional questions and comments from the interviewer. When you do this, you'll realize that you have greater control over the interview than you realize.

The goal is to create a free-flowing conversation, which is much more effective than the typical one-sided question-response format that people envision when they think of a typical interview. Keep in mind, however, that you cannot have a dialogue if you continuously ramble on; give the interviewer time to let your comments sink in so she can formulate a response.

For example, when asked for a weakness, you may

respond by saying that you are obsessive and wait for a moment before explaining further. The purpose of this dramatic pause is to let the interviewer think about what that answer means and then let her ask you to explain further. If she doesn't ask quickly, you can start explaining what you meant by your answer and provide examples.

After you have engaged the interviewer in a healthy dialogue, you can start looking for feedback by asking a question like, "What are your initial thoughts about my potential fit for the role or group?" By adding the qualifying words "initial" and "potential," you avoid putting too much pressure on the interviewer to form an opinion on the spot. Don't wait until the end of the interview to ask this question, though, because you may not have enough time to address any concerns in full. Ask for feedback sparingly during the interview because asking too often will give the impression you are insecure.

Verbal rapport-building techniques include:

- Subtly mimic your interviewer's speaking style by matching his tone, speed, and volume. Such techniques, when done in a way that is not obvious, have been shown to build trust.
- Occasionally nod as he speaks and repeat back some of what he said to preface your answer and show agreement.
- Avoid flattery. Don't mention how successful he is or compliment his suit or appearance. Even if you're being sincere, this can easily be

construed as sucking-up.

- Avoid overselling yourself. If you're overly aggressive, the interviewer may assume you're desperate or cocky.

If you are unfamiliar with these techniques, you will need to practice incorporating these skills in mock and informational interviews so they become more natural during regular interviews.

Composing Your Story

Storytelling is the oldest and most effective form of communication. Oral traditions have been used for millennia to entertain, pass on history, and instill moral values. Tapping into this primal desire to be entertained is the most effective method in making a strong, lasting impression on interviewers. They may not remember your classes or grades, but they will remember stories and anecdotes about your choices and motivations.

Most interview questions can be answered in the form of a story. For example:

- Tell me about yourself.
- What motivates you?
- Why did you choose your major?
- Why do you want to work for our company?

Stories have a beginning, middle, and end, with the middle being the most important part—the place where the action happens. This is where the drama of the narrative unfolds. Did you overcome a hardship? Learn something about yourself? Undergo a transformation? Experience a profound insight? You have a better chance of engrossing the interviewer with your story if you provide more details.

Some stories are so compelling that they tell themselves. I once hired an intern who explained how she had spent part of her childhood in a refugee camp under pretty harsh conditions. She went on to tell me that after emigrating to the U.S., she was able to attend a prestigious college and worked in retail during school to help pay for her tuition since money was tight. She was very well-spoken, and there was no question about her ability to overcome hardships and, through it all, still maintain a great attitude.

Make sure to tell your story in a unique and personal way. These days, the typical my-parents-moved-from-China/Korea/Mexico/India/Bosnia/Russia-to-the-U.S.-to-build-a-better-life-for-their-children   story has been told so many times it's almost meaningless. Plus, talking about what your parents or grandparents did and sacrificed doesn't tell us anything about you.

What you can talk about is what you learned from them and how it is relevant to your life and career. For example, "My parents forced me to take Kung Fu classes as a link to our Chinese heritage. What I learned was that some techniques that worked well against another 5'5" person usually didn't work against a determined, non-compliant 6' tall person. The instructor told me the techniques had been handed down for generations, so I just needed to train harder to make them work—they never worked. I learned that context is important and have been challenging conventional wisdom ever since."

Continuing the example above, it would have been perfectly logical for the interviewer to ask for an example of when the job candidate challenged conventional wisdom. Be prepared to provide examples of lessons learned from your stories.

The S.T.A.R. construct is also an effective construct to frame your answers to most interview questions:

- Situation—Explain the details of the challenge you or your group faced.
- Task—What was your role and goal in this situation?
- Action—Describe in detail your thought process, experience, tools, and skills used and the action taken.
- Result—What was the outcome of your action? What were the lessons learned?

We will go through examples of how to use stories to answer interview questions in Chapter 10.

Chapter 9
Interview Formats and
Types of Interviews

INTERVIEW FORMATS AND settings can vary from the typical face-to-face meeting at an office to a telephone conversation or a meeting over a meal. Depending on the setting, there are specific considerations to take into account to ensure the interview goes smoothly. We will begin by explaining the proper etiquette for the most common format, face-to-face meetings.

Formats

Face-to-Face Meeting

—Arrival Checklist:

- Arrive at least 10-15 minutes early. Check traffic reports or the status of mass transportation well in advance so you can plan for any potential delays. If you arrive more than 15 minutes before your scheduled interview time, find a place to wait until 10-15 minutes before your appointment. Checking in too

early is unprofessional because you may inadvertently interrupt the interviewer or make
her feel rushed, and neither situation creates
a good first impression.

- Greet the receptionist/assistant enthusiastically. Remember her name and address her
by name when you leave. It is a good habit
(and common courtesy) to establish rapport
with gatekeepers.

- Subtly glance at any sign-in logs to see who
else may be interviewing there. This advice
is more relevant for more experienced applicants, but it is a good habit to start early in
your career.

- Mute or turn off your mobile phone while still
in the reception area.

Confirm the time allotted for the interview with the
interviewer as soon as you sit down. Knowing how
much time you have will allow you to make sure you
get your points across. Do not check messages while
waiting for the next interviewer even if you have free
time—you want to seem eager for the position. Few
things are so important that you need to respond to
them immediately, particularly for students, so check
your messages after you leave the interview.

Some interviewers will have marked up your resume
and will ask follow-up questions, while others may
not have read it at all. Unless asked about it specifically, do not reference your resume during the interview because you want the interviewer focused
on you rather than a piece of paper. That being said,
always bring hard copies of your resume to inter-

views just in case someone asks for it.

Companies sometimes use telephone calls and video conference calls to conduct initial interviews because they are more time and cost-effective. Listed below are ideas you can use to optimize your performance for each format.

Telephone

- Smile. Even though no one can see you, smiling will make you feel more confident and will translate through on the call.
- Sit up straight in a chair at a desk to avoid slouching. Good posture ensures good breathing, which helps you sound alert.
- Don't talk too much. Because you won't be getting any visual cues or feedback, you need to pause and check for the interviewer's reactions.
- Have a copy of your resume in front of you because the interviewer will likely be looking at it, and it will help you focus on the questions being asked.
- Prepare a list of answers to common questions as well as your own questions to ask the interviewer.
- Use a corded landline if possible to ensure a good connection.
- If you are using a mobile phone, have your phone charger available, be near an electrical outlet, and make sure you are at a location where the reception is strong.
- Take notes so that you have something you

can refer back to in thank-you notes and follow-up conversations.

Video

- Dress from head-to-toe as if you were attending an in-person interview; you never know when you might have to stand up for some reason.
- Ensure sufficient lighting and a plain wall for the background because you want to avoid distractions.
- Use the picture-in-picture function to ensure you maintain a professional appearance throughout the session.
- If you are using Wi-Fi, disconnect other devices (other computers, mobile phones, Netflix, etc.) to ensure the highest possible bandwidth for your video conference.
- Close all other applications on your computer that may generate distracting notifications.

Dining

It is not uncommon for interviewers to conduct interviews over a meal. They may want to put the candidate at ease by using a less formal environment, or they may want to see how you behave in a social setting.

- Allow one of the hosts to order first and follow his lead regarding the number of courses.
- Do not order the most expensive entrees.
- Avoid ordering sloppy foods such as spaghetti, ribs, burgers, etc. Choose foods you can eat with a knife and fork.

- Avoid spinach or kale because they tend to stick to your teeth.
- Take small bites so you can respond quickly. The purpose of the meal is for the interview, not the food. Leave your meal unfinished if others have already finished their meals and just tell the server you are done.
- Make eye contact and say thank you when addressing the server.
- Avoid alcohol even if others imbibe.
- Turn off your mobile phone.
- Practice basic dining etiquette: keep elbows off of the table, use utensils from outside inwards, tear off pieces of bread and butter each piece separately, and don't season food without tasting it first.

Panel

It is common for a candidate to be interviewed by several people at the same time. This can increase the pressure in an already stressful situation, so the key is to understand the following different dynamics beforehand:

- Panel interviews are a cross between an interview and a presentation. As you answer questions, do not focus exclusively on the interviewer posing the question but also make eye contact with the other interviewers. See who is nodding in agreement as you speak and who is not. Pay special attention to those who are not and try to increase rapport by directing your focus on them a bit more.

- One of the goals of panel interviews is to see how you perform in a professional meeting. Your confidence, demeanor, and the ability to hold a crowd's attention are all being evaluated. You may be a little more animated than you would be during a one-on-one interview since you are trying to engage a larger audience with varying personalities and levels of seniority.
- Close the interview with a summary of why you are a great fit for the position.
- Follow up with each panel member individually and personalize thank-you notes by bringing up a point that person made during the interview. I will provide more advice on how to do this in Chapter 10.

Types

In addition to understanding the various interview formats, it is important to understand the different *types* of interviews used by companies to assess candidate qualifications, from preliminary screening interviews to case studies. Listed below are the most common types.

Screening

Screening interviews are usually conducted via phone by Human Resources to pre-qualify candidates before inviting them to meet with hiring managers. For the same reasons you incorporate key words from online job postings into your resume to get past electronic resume scanners, position your experience in the same language as the job posting/requirements for the screening interview. Prepare and treat screening interviews as seriously as you would a face-to-face interview because a bad first impression with HR can torpedo your candidacy.

Behavioral

—Situation, Task, Action, and Result (STAR)

As the name suggests, the goal of a behavioral interview is to gain insight into your behavior. The interviewer wants to learn how you make decisions, gain an understanding of your personality, and get a sense of your character. The focus is, therefore, less on skills and work experience and more on how your past performance can predict your future performance. The tone of these interviews is similar to a conversation with a therapist: "Can you tell me about how you dealt with a difficult team member?" "What was your role and how did you contribute to the team project?"

One of the goals of behavioral interviews is to uncover a candidate's thought processes. The interviewer will most likely delve deeper by responding to every answer you provide with: "Tell me more" and "What did you learn?" Given you know these additional probing questions are coming, consider challenging yourself to prepare comprehensive stories by asking yourself "So what?" and "Why should the interviewer care?" after each of your answers. The example below shows how to develop a logical and coherent series of answers.

Interviewer: What did you gain from your summer internship?

You: I learned a lot about game apps

and gained some great hands-on experience by helping the firm beta-test its product.

Interviewer: So what?

You: The user interface was confusing so we made changes to simplify it, which resulted in some unintended consequences and required additional revisions.

Interviewer: So what?

You: I learned the importance of regression testing to ensure that the original goals and plans are maintained as changes and improvements are incorporated. I learned how not to lose sight of the big picture even as I was mired in the intricate details of a project.

Prepare your answers to sustain at least two rounds of "So what?" This will ensure you provide enough details to leave a strong impression on the interviewer and shows you are not embellishing your qualifications or accomplishments. This is an additional facet of developing the persuasive storytelling skills described earlier.

Conversational/Informal

Informal interviews can be great because they alleviate some of the pressure you may feel in a more formal, structured setting. However, in such a case, it can be difficult to determine how and when to sell yourself for the job. You have to keep on track to ensure the interviewer doesn't spend too much time just socializing. The interviewer may not be very experienced and may end up treating the interview as more of a friendly chat. In such a scenario, it's best just to go along with the interviewer if she seems really interested in a topic, even if you can't immediately see how that interest is relevant to your candidacy.

An executive at a large publishing company recounted how he was hired for his first job out of school. The on-campus interviewer was intrigued by the student's landscaping business, which employed several workers. After going through the business' operations and financials, the interviewer made a job offer. After the student started in the position, he asked his interviewer turned manager why he was hired without any writing or publishing experience. The manager responded that he was impressed with the student's initiative and business acumen and that he didn't need a candidate with experience because he would have to train the candidate anyway.

That said, you have to be careful that the interviewer doesn't go so far off-topic that you are unable to close the interview. Try diplomatically to steer the conversation back to your story and show how your traits, experience, and motivations are a great fit with the company's needs. If two or three sets of questions and answers have convinced you that the interview needs to be redirected, there are several tactics you can try depending on the stage of the interview:

- "If it's okay with you…."
- "Just to be considerate of our time constraints…."
- "I would like to go into some more detail about

[a position or academic choice]…" to explain how a skill or previous experience is relevant for the position you are applying for.

Case Studies

In a case study interview format, the candidate is presented with a business scenario, such as how to improve profitability or whether a merger or acquisition makes sense. He will be asked to provide a solution based on analytical and quantitative skills, communications, business insight, and creativity within a short time limit. The problem can also be a brain-teaser, such as being asked to determine how many gas stations there are in the country. Sometimes, a small group of candidates will be asked to work on a problem together to assess their teamwork.

You should be able to ask the interviewer for additional information about the business scenario. Taking time to think through your questions so you can ask insightful ones provides an additional opportunity to differentiate yourself from other candidates. Listen for cues in the interviewer's answers to see how this new information will help you formulate your solution or recommendation. You can also "think out loud" to see whether the interviewer provides further guidance as you talk through your assumptions and analysis.

There is typically no single correct answer to these questions; the interviewer is really only interested in finding out how you think and solve problems. Even if you don't provide the perfect answer, you can still be viewed favorably if you are able to analyze the problem and articulate the steps you took to arrive at your conclusion.

Chapter 10
Acing the Interview

Y OUR NETWORKING EFFORTS and all the time you spent perfecting your resume and cover letter has paid off; you have been granted an interview. This is your opportunity to convince the company that you are the right candidate for the position.

The first part of this chapter explains the purpose behind many common questions, so you can prepare answers to address the interviewer's true concerns. In keeping with the strategy of differentiating yourself from other candidates, the goal is to provide interesting and uncommon answers to these common questions. The second part of the chapter focuses on preparing insightful questions to ask the interviewer to create the best possible impression. The last section explains how to follow up after the interview.

It is worth pointing out that many students I have advised have expressed concerns that their experiences and activities were not particularly noteworthy and that it was challenging to make them sound impressive. My response was that a significant number of their classmates shared the same concerns, so they should not feel insecure about their accomplishments. Students can still make a strong impression if they are able to convey to interviewers how their experiences affected their career decisions and aspirations. Interviewers are more likely to empathize with candidates who personalize their stories.

Interviewer Questions: Open-Ended

"Tell me about yourself." Translation: "How do your experiences and motivations translate into traits and behaviors we value, and how can you help us reach our goals?"

An open-ended question like this one doesn't have one specific answer and, therefore, allows you to tell your story your way. However, unlike experienced professionals who can point to their relevant professional accomplishments, first-time job seekers have the more challenging task of using their academic and extracurricular successes to demonstrate that they possess traits and skills that would be useful to the company. Keep your answers short, about a minute to a minute and a half, focusing on the two or three most important points you need to convey.

Use an anecdote to explain why you chose your field. As explained earlier, the "why" engages the interviewer on an emotional level, helping you establish a stronger connection. Next, point out accomplishments and activities that highlight skills useful to the company. Interviewers are also gauging whether they will want to sit next to you for eight to ten hours a day. Don't recount your entire life story, but do begin or end your answer with a personal point. The final point should be crafted to lead to follow-up questions from the interviewer.

Here's an example of a good answer:

"During high school, I used to bond with my father at the local Off-Track-Betting parlor. I wasn't old enough to gamble, but my father would place bets for me with the money I earned from working odd jobs. This is why finance and trading seemed like the perfect major for me to pursue in college. After taking a few finance courses, I realized that I was able to pursue my interest in math and apply it to the field of finance. I enjoyed being on a nationally-ranked math team in high school and had wondered how that would translate into a career. The answer for me was in financial derivatives, which require strong quantitative skills, so it is a perfect fit. I am also getting a minor in Classical Studies with a focus on Norse mythology, though, unfortunately, the school does not have that as a minor."

There are a few reasons why this is a great answer to the question "Tell me about yourself." The candidate included a little bit of humor by telling the betting story (most parents aren't gambling "enablers" for their children), conveyed strong analytical skills by pointing to experience on a top math team, and explained why his area of interest was a good fit for his skills and personality. By ending with an unrelated comment about his interest in mythology, the candidate provides an easy follow-up question for the interviewer, who will likely now ask how he became interested in mythology, allowing him to explain his background further.

Here's another good example:

"I am an only child, so I guess I grew up getting a lot of attention. Both of my parents were academics, my father in engineering and my mother in biology, so they were surprised that my interest was in writing, but they were both very supportive. I joined the school newspaper in my first year and wrote about everything from the political biases of the faculty (which I determined based on their political contributions) to a review of the local Mongolian restaurant. We were up until four in the morning every night before the twice-a-week publishing deadline. The experience was intense, but through the process, I know I made some friends for life. I was fortunate to be elected managing editor for the paper in my sophomore year, which was great confirmation that my work was well-respected by my peers. I also enjoy posting on my blog, which I do almost daily."

This answer demonstrates the student's dedication to the job and that she is likely a team player because she mentioned the respect of peers as an important point. The mention of working until four in the morning, which would typically not be included in a resume, is important to share in the interview. The last point is a nice hook to continue the conversation, as the next likely question from the interviewer is, "What do you blog about?"

Here's an example of a weak answer:

"I have always had a big-picture perspective, which is why I am attracted to management consulting and excited about the opportunity to work on strategic initiatives with C-suite executives. I want to be able to contribute to something impactful early in my career. McKinsey has produced more Fortune 500 CEOs than any other organization in the world. The skills from this career are very useful across industries, and it is a great way to build industry expertise. Having an inside view across multiple companies provides a unique and very broad perspective, as if you had worked at all of these companies."

This response sounds like it was written for a recruiting brochure, using a lot of buzzwords but not detailing anything personal about the candidate or conveying information about the candidate's value to potential employers.

Another popular, open-ended interview query is, "Walk me through your resume." Translation: "What would you like me to know about you that isn't on your resume?"

Assume the interviewer has already read your resume, so don't repeat your academic and professional achievements listed there. The interviewer already has the "whats" and now wants to understand the "hows" and the "whys." She wants to know your motivations for making the choices you made:

- How did you find your part-time jobs, summer jobs, and research positions? Were there any obstacles you had to overcome to gain these positions?

- Were there any surprises/obstacles you encountered while on the job? What did you learn from them?
- What did you learn about your role or the industry that excites you and confirms your desire to enter this industry?
- Does your college offer something in particular that drove your decision to go there?

Incorporate anecdotes to demonstrate lessons learned or motivating factors, adding the specific details of your experiences. For example:

- "My job at McDonald's taught me that smart and hardworking people come from all walks of life."
- "My summer roofing job in Phoenix, where it reached 110 degrees most days, taught me I wanted to go to college instead of working in the roofing business."
- "From my internship at company X, I learned that being early and prepared is half the battle for success. I got into the office early and was able to chat informally with senior members of the team before the day became too hectic."
- "I was choosing between internships at company A and company B during the summer of my sophomore year and chose B because cold-calling customers was outside of my comfort zone and it would force me to deal with my shyness. By the end of the summer, the initial dread I used to experience before

picking up the phone had been replaced by a feeling of calm, and I no longer have any fear or trepidation."

"What do you know about our company?" Translation: "Can you demonstrate, through your efforts to learn about the company, how much you really want to work for our company?"

The answer to this question needs to show the interviewer how proactive you have been in learning about the company, which is just as, if not more important than the actual information you learned about the company. Overwhelm the interviewer with your demonstrated interest. Start by describing the people you have met in the company through informational interviews. Mention that you signed up to receive press releases and RSS feeds, and that you read industry periodicals and research reports from brokerage firms that discussed the company. Then, focus on the results of your research efforts and explain why you are a good fit for the company. The answer to the question, "Why do you want to work for us?" is explained later in this chapter and will help you explain your fit.

Interviewer Questions: Personality

"What are your key strengths?"

Strengths and weaknesses can be broken down into two categories: intrinsic personality traits, which can be managed but generally not changed, and skills, which can be developed and improved over time. Personality traits are less suited to mention as weaknesses because they are more difficult to improve upon. For this same reason, traits are great to list as strengths because they are part of your being and unlikely to change much. Examples of traits would be "I'm an introvert" or "I'm a natural born leader." Examples of weak skills may include, "I lack experience with social media marketing techniques" or "I don't have much experience negotiating."

Answer the strengths question with traits that are not commonly given as answers to it. For example, "I have an infectious passion for the topics I am interested in. People can sense that and are quick to respond to it, so I view it as a leadership trait. I was able to increase membership in the entrepreneurship club by 45 percent after I gave the recruiting presentation for the club, turning around a decline in membership."

Other traits include:

- A sense of urgency: "I was the go-to person for previous managers because I was trusted to get the job done."
- Intellectual curiosity (personal or academic): "This is why I selected an interesting research topic."
- Contrarian viewpoints: "I find this helps me provide additional perspectives when brainstorming."
- A consensus builder: "I focus on addressing individual concerns in order to find common ground."
- Empathy: "I am able to work well with all personality types."

Emotional Intelligence (or Emotional Quotient) is the ability to understand your emotions and manage them, as well as the ability to decode the emotional information of others and act accordingly, taking that information into account to achieve a common goal.

Even if you aren't interviewing for a sales position, sales skills can be pitched as a strength because the ability to influence or persuade others is a valuable skill for any position. If you use sales skills as a strength, be prepared to sell something to the interviewer because you may be asked to demonstrate your sales acumen. A classic example is when the interviewer asks the candidate to try to sell him a pen. You can start by saying the pen will allow you to express your feelings or convey a thought because it is foremost a communications tool. Then you can go on to explain its benefits, such as the fact that, unlike a computer or phone, it doesn't need batteries.

This is not typical advice from career coaches, but the strengths question is an opportunity to have some fun and show your humorous side. I didn't get the strengths/weaknesses question too often in the latter part of my career, but my response to the strengths question is a combination of intellectual curiosity and a short attention span. It is another way of saying, "I stay fresh by continually trying new things." Those traits led to my career in two global industries across three continents over a thirty-year period, affording my children the opportunity to visit two dozen countries before they began high school.

"What is your biggest weakness?"

Controlled honesty is the guiding principle for answering the weakness question. The challenge is that there is little upside in any answer you provide. You want to avoid sounding disingenuous by saying, "I work too hard," or "I demand too much of myself and others." Interviewers have heard all of these self-serving answers before and are turned off by them.

You can use this opportunity to demonstrate self-awareness; a weakness can be as simple as a lack of practical experience in the field. You don't have the proven track record, but you are confident you have the attitude and training to succeed. Prepare a story or anecdote to highlight a trait to emphasize your point.

Alternatively, you can choose a non-core competency as a skill weakness and explain your plans to improve. If you have a technical role, you can say you are working on improving your financial acumen; if you are a finance major, you can point out a need to improve technical skills, such as learning a high-level scripting language. Other weaknesses could be a fear of public speaking, lack of experience in negotiating, no client-facing or customer service experience—all skills which can be improved.

If you prefer to discuss trait weaknesses, examples would include:

- Impatient (but you're learning to be more empathetic by stepping back and trying to understand the other person's perspective).

- Obsessive (but you're working on improving time management because of it).
- Abrupt with people who don't share your same sense of urgency (but you're trying to develop a better poker face so your irritation doesn't show and you can get everyone onboard).
- Stubborn (because you have strong convictions and always come prepared to back them up).
- Unassertive (but you're learning that, in brainstorming sessions, your idea doesn't have to be completely fleshed out before you propose it).
- Dislike confrontation (which you know can be mistaken for not having confidence in yourself or your ideas, so you're practicing speaking up and advocating for yourself and others).

"What was the biggest obstacle or challenge you overcame?"

Obstacles or struggles can be personal or professional. Explain how the obstacle disadvantaged you, and then explain how you overcame this obstacle and what traits surfaced as a result.

For example: "Only after performing poorly in middle school for several years was I finally properly diagnosed with a mild form of dyslexia. It took several more years for me to learn how to work with this learning disability, but I was able to graduate high school in the top 10 percent of my class. I will always have to work a bit harder than others because of the dyslexia, but it also gives me the motivation to prove that I can be as good as anyone else."

Another example: "I was overweight as a child, which led to shyness because I didn't want to draw attention to myself. I didn't speak in class and mostly kept to myself with the exception of a few close friends. I don't remember the exact moment, but in my sophomore year in high school, I decided I was tired of being fat. I took small steps by starting with a few push-ups and reducing the comfort snacking. After a year, I had lost twenty-five pounds and I engaged in regular exercise, even completing a 10K run. I became much more confident and outgoing as I realized I was not inherently shy, but I was just apprehensive about speaking out previously."

"What was your biggest failure?"

The failure question is related to the previous obstacle/challenge question, the difference being that obstacles occur through no fault of your own while failures are a direct result of your actions. Both questions are asked to determine your resilience. Getting rejected from a college or doing badly in a class is not necessarily material and is pretty commonplace.

Failures should be based on an activity in which you invested a significant amount of time and that had a material effect on you. The context is important to crafting a compelling narrative. For example, you had to change majors because you couldn't "cut it." This was a harsh realization because you had a 4.0 GPA in high school and you were always successful academically. The lesson learned is that failure is a single outcome of a single event; as long as you don't define yourself by it, and you are able to move on, you'll be fine.

Other examples of failure can include:

- Missed making a team after significant training and effort.
- Lost a championship game (which you were favored to win).
- Was let go or fired from a part-time job when you were young because you didn't take the role seriously or showed up late too many times. (With an answer like this, be sure to point out that you were young and learned a valuable lesson from this experience.)

The most important point of your answer is to convey how the experience made you stronger. The revelation can be the realization that the world doesn't care how badly you want something, but rather, it's the effort you put in that gives you a chance to succeed.

"What motivates you?" Translation: "What are your values and goals?"

The answer to this question is based on the earlier discussion about fit in the "Finding Your Fit" section of Chapter 1. The strategy is to position your values and goals so that the interviewer can relate to them and help you follow or achieve them. I say "position your values and goals" because it's not enough to state them; you need to frame them in a way that is relevant to the company's interests. For example, everyone can understand the desire for financial security for oneself and one's family, especially if you grew up in a home where money was tight. However, stating you want to make a lot of money creates the impression that the only reason you want the job is for the paycheck when, in reality, it could just mean that you're willing to work hard to ensure your financial well-being.

If you are interested in a design or marketing role, your answer could be that you are a creative person, so it is important to you that your job allows you to express your creativity. You need to be able to substantiate your creativity with examples such as a portfolio of your work or a blog. The interviewer should be able to relate to that need and will likely reassure you that you will definitely have the opportunity to express your creativity. Here you have created a situation in which the interviewer has confirmed to you (and herself) that your goals can be fulfilled within the company. Thus, this company is going to be a good fit.

"What is your greatest accomplishment?" is similar to the previous question on motivations since the interviewer is gauging what is important to you.

The answer should specify why the accomplishment is important to you. Avoid clichés such as being admitted to a top university, especially if it is an on-campus interview because everyone being interviewed got into the school, so this answer doesn't differentiate you. Did you overcome a phobia—which can be the basis of an engaging story?

Another example might be an athletic achievement that required you to balance academics and athletics to attain a ranking or championship. This answer shows commitment and the resulting, specific achievement. The answer can also be gaining a competitive research position that ignited your interest in the field because of the specific project or professor.

Example of a good answer:

"I had cold-called a brokerage firm and was able to secure a part-time position there during the school year. This job was very important because much of what I was reading in the textbooks and hearing in lectures seemed very theoretical, and I was pretty confused about how that information could be useful. Only after I started working with the traders was I able to understand which information I had learned in school was practical and which was not. This was confirmed later when an interviewer said I knew more about the business than all of the other candidates combined. In hindsight, I view getting this job as my greatest accomplishment so far because it confirmed that finance is the career I want to pursue."

This response highlights several traits: initiative to cold-call and gain a position, the tenacity to work during the school year, the common sense to realize some of the coursework didn't seem useful.

"Can you give an example of when you led/worked on a team and when you overcame a difficult team situation?"

Examples of teamwork and leadership can be from any activity: academic, professional, or extracurricular. Leadership is not a function or position but rather a behavior that influences perception and then affects behavior. It is different than management, which is a role or function within a hierarchy. Understanding this difference opens up more possibilities to show how you were able to influence the viewpoints and behaviors of others because you don't need to have been a captain or manager to have been a leader. It is important to point out your individual contribution and leadership in the context of the team's overall success.

- What objections or resistance did you have to overcome?
- Why did people have those concerns?
- How were you able to persuade others to come around to your viewpoint? Examples include: explaining the risk/reward, leading by example, empathizing, cajoling, or applying peer pressure.

I am sure everyone has had to overcome issues working on a group project for school, so that is probably the best place to find a scenario to answer this question. For example, team members may not be equally motivated to complete a computer science project. For some, the project may not be within their major; others may be taking the course as a pass/fail, so they are less concerned about the grade. How did you resolve this type of situation?

"Describe your perfect job." Translation: "Are your expectations realistic and a good fit for our organization?"

You can construct the "perfect job" answer to reinforce your personal brand. Avoid the nondescript generalities about being a contributing member of a team, learning from more experienced professionals, or being in a dynamic environment that challenges you every day. The answer should be specific and describe the ideal environment you want to work in, the people you want to interact with, and what you expect to do day-to-day. Then, show your ambition by explaining the level of responsibility and autonomy you would like, such as client or project responsibility, without being micro-managed. The exact answers depend on the industry and your role in it.

For example, if you are interested in a sales position, you can explain that you want a level of responsibility, such as being the account manager for eight to twelve strategic clients. You also want access to sufficient corporate resources so you can strike a good balance between working with clients and the internal team to solve client issues and problems. Because you are on the front lines dealing with clients every day, your input should be a factor in product development, so it is important your voice is heard in that process.

"What are your hobbies?" Translation: "Are you the type of person I want to sit next to for eight to ten hours a day?"

This question is about personality and professional fit. Are you well-rounded and capable of working in a diverse environment with ever-changing tasks? You don't want to come across as if you are solely focused on your career because you will be viewed as one-dimensional and likely to burn out. Use this opportunity to build on your brand further by mentioning a few hobbies that convey positive traits about you. A few good examples:

- Reading: What are you reading right now and why do you find it interesting? Has it taught you anything or provided any insight that could apply to your role within the company?
- Educational activities like learning a new language or mindfulness meditation: these show intellectual curiosity and a desire to learn.
- Team sports: competitive or not, these demonstrate your ability to work with others and socialize in groups.

Interviewer Questions: Challenging

"Why do you want to work for us?" is related to the "What do you know about our company?" question because you want to work for the company based on what you know about it.

Avoid generic responses such as "the exciting work environment," "the company is a proven leader in the industry" or that you "love the people you've met and you feel it is a perfect fit you." This may all be true, but it doesn't tell the interviewer anything about you or your views.

"This position would look good on my resume." That was an actual response by a VP-level candidate when asked why he was interested in the position. This response was particularly embarrassing for me because I had referred this candidate to the company. Interviewers want to find dedicated and driven people for their groups, not someone who is explicitly using the role as a stepping stone for his career.

You need to do some research to answer this question without sounding clichéd. Use informational interviews at the company, industry periodicals, or the company's own statements to learn which specific product area or client demographic the company is targeting for the highest growth. Then prepare to explain two or three specific reasons why you want to be part of that vision—your goal is to show that your views are in line with those of the company and, therefore, you are a good fit for the job. Your answer should also demonstrate the detailed research you did on the company, which proves your interest in working for it. Your story is more convincing when it is supported by specific details.

For example, if you are a candidate at a consumer product company that is expanding into China, you should not say you want to work for that company because China has a growing middle class with increasing discretionary income. That is common knowledge and doesn't show any insight. Dig deeper into the specifics to provide context and demonstrate your insights; is the target demographic returning professionals who were educated and worked overseas and are now concerned about the quality and safety of local products? Or is the target market locals of a specific age group and professional demographic who want to embrace Western culture to be seen as more cosmopolitan? Show evidence to support your view, such as the increased spending for foreign luxury goods and high end French wines by this target group. Companies are very specific about defining their target markets, and your answers will be more impressive if you are able to speak their language.

There are only a few situations in which the question "Why do you want to work for us?" can be successfully answered with "Because of the corporate culture." For example, if you are interested in scientific research and the management team and board of directors at this company includes many scientists, rather than being dominated by business and finance professionals, the answer may work. It will only be an effective answer if you can point out specific ways in which this company's culture differs from its competition.

"Why are you the best candidate?" Translation: "What makes you unique?" or "Why should we hire you?"

This question is somewhat unfair because you don't know the other people being interviewed, but there are still a few rules to follow when answering it. First, don't denigrate others. You can say, "There are probably a lot of qualified candidates" (which shows you are not arrogant), or simply "I can't speak about other candidates because I don't know them." Then, you can explain why you are the right candidate; there is no single right answer, but this is another opportunity to reinforce your brand, explain your strengths and motivations, and substantiate your claims with behavioral examples and anecdotes.

Example of a strong answer:

"My confidence is one of the most important assets I can bring to the company. I can be truly confident because I know I have really 'done my homework' and worked as hard as anyone else to achieve my goals. For example, I was a finalist for a national science contest because I was able to get to school by 5:30 a.m., after an hour-long train ride, to work on my project before the school officially opened. My biology teacher was an inspiration because she met me on these early mornings to open the school and the lab so I could work on the project before classes began. My technical qualifications also make me a good fit for the digital marketing position; I helped increase website traffic 20 percent at my last internship by improving the metadata and alt tags."

Interviewer Questions: Professional

"Where do you see yourself in five or ten years?" Translation: "How realistic are your ambitions?"

"President of the company!" is unlikely to get you the job offer. Your answer should show the interviewer that your career goals are aggressive but realistic so you will come across as manageable. Career progression will vary significantly by industry, but the characteristics of your answer should include specific increases in autonomy and responsibility for your role so the interviewer can see that you expect to provide assistance to your manager and add value to the company.

For example, for a sales position, a good answer might be that you expect account responsibility for larger and strategic clients at year five, after you've proven yourself by bringing in new clients and up-selling existing clients. By year ten, you expect to become a producing sales manager, whereby you are managing and developing junior salespeople but still have some direct client responsibility to maintain an understanding of client concerns. This answer shows that you expect to earn greater responsibility and not have it handed to you purely because of the passage of time, which demonstrates maturity and also helps to dispel concerns about a sense of entitlement.

"How would a previous manager describe you?" Translation: "Are you aware of how other people perceive you?"

This question is not meant to be a trap, so don't turn it into one by complaining about a previous manager or employer. Use controlled honesty and focus on the positives that will present you as an attractive employee. "Former managers would describe me as low maintenance and just focused on doing whatever it took to get the job done without any drama. They would also say I have great attention to detail/am creative in finding solutions/play well with others/am the first to volunteer for tasks. They would probably sum up their views of me by saying they would be happy to hire me again." List a few strong points, but don't overdo it; otherwise, it will sound contrived.

Be prepared to give examples since the interviewer will surely ask for them. Provide the examples in the typical Situation, Task, Activity, and Result framework to convey a complete story. Also, review the earlier section, "Concerns of Hiring Managers," since this is the perfect situation to show the interviewer indirectly how you can address his concerns directly.

"How would former colleagues describe you?"

This question is very similar to the previous one, so the same strategies apply. "Former colleagues would describe me as energetic and always willing to lend a hand. They would also say that I am empathetic and made an extra effort to understand other people's viewpoints. Finally, they enjoyed working with me as they appreciated my self-deprecating humor and the fact that I didn't take myself too seriously." This question affords you the opportunity to describe your soft skills and Emotional Quotient (EQ). Saying that former colleagues fawned over your intelligence and technical skills is not a useful answer because it is difficult to go into further details without sounding self-serving.

Interviewer Questions: Academic

Academic questions can range from technical to subjective and can vary dramatically depending on your major. If you are a computer science major or minor, you may be asked to diagram a software problem or write code to solve a problem; in this competitive technical environment, even people with more than twenty years of programming experience are being asked to write code in interviews.

You may be asked to explain a financial concept such as duration, a statistical concept such as a standard deviation, or the meaning of iambic pentameter. These are all fair questions if they are within your area of study. As an electrical engineering student, I once had an interview in which the interviewer laid out an electrical schematic he was working on and asked me to determine the voltages at random points of the circuitry. That was fair game even though I completely flubbed the answer.

If you don't know the answer to an academic question, at least try to get "partial credit" by working through the problem as far as you can to show your thought process. You should feel free to ask questions for clarification at any point as you try to answer the question. If you get stuck, explain why you are stuck; then the interviewer may provide you with a hint to help you work through it.

If you can't answer the question directly, another possible strategy is to explain the answer's context. For example, I was asked for the formula for a proprietary statistical function and responded by explaining when the function should be used, how it was used, and why it was used, even though I didn't remember the exact equation. Even if you are not able to answer the question directly, you can show a practical understanding of the principles—which the interviewer should take into account in assessing you.

"What was your most/least favorite course at school and why?"

Be creative about how a course affected you or gave you a different perspective rather than simply explaining what you learned. A finance professor at my business school came into class one day and started writing a long equation on the board. When he finished, he explained that given the number of investment managers in the United States and the distribution of returns from the market, there should, statistically speaking, be at least one or two people in the country with long-term, consistent outsized returns like those Warren Buffet produces; it just happens to be Warren Buffet. As an engineer, this professor's analytical view of the world thoroughly resonated with me.

You might not enjoy a course because of the subject matter or the professor/lecturer. Perhaps the material was too theoretical and lacked real world applications. Or maybe it was not sufficiently challenging, but you realized this too late to drop it. The presenter was monotonic and didn't provide any additional insight beyond what the textbook provided. Don't make it a personal issue, by complaining that, for instance, the professor picked on or graded you unfairly.

Interviewer Questions: Brainteasers

Brainteasers are typically used in the finance, technology, and management consulting industries because they allow interviewers to evaluate a candidate's thought process and logic skills. Whether they actually predict how well a candidate will do on the job is debatable, but you may be confronted with brain teasers, so it is worth doing some preparation.

Categories include quantitative questions with a single correct answer, logic questions that can have multiple possible answers, and analytical questions that evaluate reasoning skills.

An example of a quantitative question is: "If you stacked 1,000 cubes into a 10x10x10 configuration and painted all of the exposed sides of the cubes, how many of the 1,000 cubes are left completely unpainted?" Another example is: "When a certain type of lily pad is introduced into a pond, it doubles every day and takes sixty-four days to fill the pond completely. How many days does it take to fill half the pond?" Probability and statistical questions are also popular for this category, for example: "From a deck of playing cards, what are the odds of picking two clubs and then a heart?" Or, from a pair of dice, "What are the odds of rolling the sum of eight, three times in a row?"

The classic logic question is, "Why are manhole covers round?" Possible answers are "Because they can't fall into the manhole" or "They are easier to move by rolling them." Another popular question is, "There are nine metal balls that look identical, but one is slightly heavier than the other eight. You are permitted to use a balance scale, twice. How do you determine the heavier ball?"

Market sizing and guesstimate questions are used to evaluate candidates' analytical and reasoning skills. For example: "How many tennis courts are there in the United States?" or "How many tennis balls would fit in the Empire State Building?" The basic strategy here is to break the problem down into smaller units, make assumptions based on smaller units, lay out each assumption and other options, and extrapolate to answer the original question. Before answering, have a quick sanity check to see whether your result is plausible. For example, given that the U.S. population is about 320 million people, it's unlikely there are 100 million tennis courts (one for every 3.2 people) in the country.

What NOT to Say in Interviews

Avoid using any slang since that may be viewed as unprofessional.

Do not share any confidential information about past employers. That will signal to the interviewer that you may not be trustworthy. After all, if you are willing to disclose proprietary data about one employer, what would stop you from disclosing such data about another?

As tempting as it might be to vent your frustrations, don't say anything negative about previous or current employers or bosses. Some interviewers may try to goad you into complaining about a past employer, but do not fall into that trap.

Do not ask about compensation or benefits during an initial interview. These topics are much more appropriate to discuss toward the end of the recruiting process.

It's fine if an interviewer brings up work/life balance as a discussion point, but you should not be the one raising the issue. There is a risk an interviewer may not view you as sufficiently committed to the job if you ask about balance during the interview. Raise the point after you get the offer, if this issue is important to you; then you can decide whether the company is a good fit after taking into account all aspects of the position.

Overcoming Objections

An interviewer may raise an objection directly with you in an interview. Determine whether the objection is valid and a legitimate cause for concern. Objections can include a lack of direct experience or fewer technical skills than other applicants. If the objection is valid:

- Acknowledge the objection.
- Re-focus/re-define the concern.
- Demonstrate that the concern can be mitigated by your strengths, skills, or experience.

Sometimes, objections are requests for more information rather than a dismissal of your candidacy because your story is incomplete. Turn objections into opportunities to demonstrate communications skills and complete your story. For example:

Interviewer: You are applying for a marketing job, but your major is comparative literature. I don't think this is a good fit.

Response: I understand your concerns, but many of the practical skills needed are taught on the job and not learned in school. I do possess the soft skills and determination/motivation required to be successful in the position as I have demonstrated from my experience in increasing the school club membership by 325 percent in two years.

If you feel the objection is not valid, then in a diplomatic manner, explain why, in your view, given the job specifications/requirements, the objection is either not relevant or inaccurate, and redirect the conversation toward other qualities/strengths that reinforce your qualifications.

Interviewer: I don't see that you have the outgoing personality needed for this sales position.

Response: Just as there are different types of clients, I think there are different types of personalities that can be successful in a sales career. Active listening skills, the ability to convey the value of products or services, and building trust and rapport are all important aspects of a good salesperson.

In either situation, provide explanations, not excuses, because excuses deny responsibility and are more emotional and defensive. Both are signs of weakness.

How to Use Humor

While I was in business school, I interviewed for a derivatives position at an investment bank and was asked three brain teasers. I was able to answer the first two, but I was stumped by the final one. After about ten seconds of silence, the interviewer told me to feel free to think out loud. After another fifteen seconds, he reminded me it was okay to think out loud. I responded, "I am." He laughed and I made it to the next round. I think it was because I was able to answer the first two questions relatively easily and got a "pass" on the third one for my funny response.

Humor is a great way to build rapport, particularly self-deprecating humor, since it allows the interviewer to feel more at ease. The ability to laugh at yourself is also a sign of confidence. That said, you have to be careful because humor is subjective and you don't want to overdo it. Saying "My math skills are about the same level as those of a fifth grader" may be true, but it is not a fact you want to highlight in an interview (or any other setting). Also, keep in mind that what is funny for one person may be offensive to another. Definitely avoid any reference to race, religion, sex, sexual preference, or any other protected classes. Err on the side of caution if you are unsure.

You may be asked by the interviewer to tell a joke, so make sure you have one in mind before going into interviews. To be safe and avoid offending the interviewer, your joke should be funny and appropriate for a twelve-year-old child. Also, be ready to answer questions about your favorite song, movie, or book. As explained earlier, the hiring decision is more than just about qualifications for the job. The interviewer is trying to learn more about you and whether your personality is a good fit for the team.

Candidate Questions

In speaking with hiring managers across many industries, just about all of them tell me that they are more impressed by insightful questions candidates ask them than the answers candidates give to questions they're asked. This is not to say that it is not important to provide differentiating answers to interviewers' questions because it most definitely is. Rather, it is to highlight the fact that many candidates do not realize the importance of the questions they ask interviewers, and sometimes, they treat the questions as a formality at the end of the interview. This time is perhaps the best opportunity to distinguish yourself from other candidates. Questions should show thoughtfulness, research, and some meaningful effort in order to make a strong positive impression. Don't ask questions for which the answers can be found on the company website or annual reports; this shows you haven't done your homework.

"Ask thoughtful questions" is common advice from school career services offices and career websites. They then go on to suggest mundane questions, such as:

- What are your expectations for new employees?
- What are the opportunities for advancement?
- Where do you see the company in the next few years?
- What is the corporate culture like?
- What do you enjoy most about your job?
- What do you find most challenging?
- Why did you join the company?
- Who is your biggest competitor?

How thoughtful are these questions, really? They are so generic they are almost rhetorical, and they can apply to any interviewer or company. They require no effort on the part of the candidate to prepare because they can be found on countless websites.

Let's analyze several commonly suggested candidate questions that, on the surface, may sound thoughtful:

- What is a typical day like?
- What are the characteristics of successful candidates?
- If I were hired, what do you expect from me in the first ninety days?

A key concept that comes into play here is—

Not Wrong ≠ Right.

It can be argued that the questions above aren't wrong because:

- What is a typical day like?—Demonstrates interest in the role.
- What are the characteristics of successful candidates?—Attempts to solicit characteristics so the student can promote her candidacy with examples of how she embodies these characteristics.
- If I were hired, what do you expect from me in the first ninety days?—Demonstrates a pro-active, company-centric attitude.

However, interviewers have heard these generic questions many times before and will provide generic responses:

- What is a typical day like?—"No day is typical as we are a very dynamic organization and immediately respond to changes from our clients and changes in the industry."
- What are the characteristics of successful candidates?—"Smart, hardworking, honest, takes initiative, self-motivated."
- If I were hired, what do you expect from me in the first ninety days?—"Meet people you'll be working with, in and outside of our department, learn our systems, read up on our products, services, and clients…."

I am sure many interviewers may find such questions thoughtful and perfectly fine, and many candidates have received job offers after asking these questions. By the same logic, people can also live long lives despite eating poorly and not exercising, but that doesn't mean it's the best choice either. In today's job market, "just good enough" will not land you the job.

The question you need to ask yourself is, "How will the interviewer react to the questions I ask?" The ideal reactions you want to evoke from your interviewer are either, "Wow, that was a really insightful question!" or "I never thought about it that way." None of the questions above will elicit those responses.

Prepare several types of questions to get positive reactions from the interviewer:

- Strategic and Analytical: Show you have done your homework with insights on industry trends, competitive analysis, or potential disruptive technologies.
- Rapport Building: Personalize the conversation and build rapport by asking questions about the interviewer's experiences.
- Challenging: Ask questions that require the interviewer to think about areas of improvement for the company.
- Personal Growth: Demonstrate ambition while simultaneously acknowledging you have a lot to learn.

Do not preface any questions with, "This may be a silly question…" or any other statement that discounts the value of what you're asking. This is another example of negotiating against yourself and displaying a lack of confidence.

Candidate Questions: Strategic and Analytical

Ask big picture questions instead of overly specific ones that may be difficult for anyone to answer (your goal is not to trip up the interviewer) and offer your own analysis for the interviewer's opinion. Asking multiple, related questions shows that you have made an effort to think through some possibilities. This is analogous to not asking your manager a question without also suggesting possible solutions.

For example, mention a recent acquisition, divestiture, or merger at the company. Then ask whether it has had a positive or negative effect on the department or division for which you are interviewing. Which groups are the beneficiaries and which are the losers? The answers to these questions depend on the merger's purpose.

Prepare questions as if you were a business consultant hired by the company. What would you ask management to help the company figure out its product or service strategy? For example:

- How have specific mergers or acquisitions of competitors affected the company's strategy or position in the market?
- Where is the company planning to expand, and how will it differentiate itself from existing competition in those areas?

While you should not ask questions that you could have found answers to on the company's website or in its annual reports, you can still use the website and annual reports as sources of information to help you construct questions. For example:

- Look for trends across time in the company's annual reports. You can point out positive trends and ask how they were accomplished. For instance, what factors led to improving gross margins?
- If there was consistent growth in a particular division over time, ask what roles are the best opportunities for new grads with your background.

Your questions can be based on either macro trends or more specific sector issues. "Increasing energy costs means that it's less cost-effective to outsource manufacturing abroad because of the transportation costs. Are there plans to return to domestic production?" "How has the dramatic decline in oil prices over the past year affected strategies?" "Retail sales should increase as consumers have more disposable income; however, department stores and large retailers are closing down in droves. Why?" "Why have certain brick-and-mortar stores been able to buck the trend and expand?"

The fact that Millennials now outnumber Baby Boomers requires companies to alter their business models radically or else risk going out of business. Millennials expect free services and trials before deciding whether to pay for them; this applies to everything from streaming music to investment services. You can come up with so many strategic questions if you just put some thought into it and do a little research.

Through research, you can discover sector-specific

topics that allow you to engage the interviewer in a spirited discussion and create a lasting effect. The key to this strategy is to focus on second-order effects, which means that other candidates are less likely to discuss these topics. For example, if you are interviewing at Google and you are interested in its self-driving car development, know that most people will focus on the technologies, such as the cameras, sensors, and image processing, that allow the cars to work. Meanwhile, people are just beginning to discuss the ethical and legal ramifications of such technology. You can ask the interviewer, "Which area in Google is discussing the ethical ramifications of self-driving cars? For example, how does the computer program decide whether to strike three pedestrians suddenly crossing the road or swerve and strike an embankment, which may seriously injure the passengers in the car?"

An additional benefit of doing your research may be that you discover areas that pique your interest.

Candidate Questions: Rapport Building

Step one in building rapport is getting people to talk about themselves and think about their own success, which most people love to do. Step two is to tie the question to yourself—How would this person's experience help me with my career?

Questions you can ask are:

- What did you find most challenging when you began at the company/in the industry? Is this issue still relevant for someone like me starting out in the industry today?

- If you were made president of the company tomorrow, what three things would you change immediately?
- How would you compare this company to others you have worked for? What are the pros and cons of working here versus somewhere else?

Candidate Questions: Challenging

One challenge in interviews is getting an honest picture of a company's weaknesses. Everyone assumes interviewers will avoid expressing any negativity about their organizations, but this is not always the case. When presented in the right way, challenging questions can help you gain important insight into your future employer. And besides, you may not want to work for someone who isn't truthful with you about some of the company's less-than-perfect aspects.

The following examples are challenging questions that require confidence to ask. However, they are truly insightful questions that will engage interviewers at a much deeper level because they will have to think through atypical scenarios. You may want to preface or caveat these types of questions with statements such as, "To understand better the culture/priorities/growth opportunities/challenges here..."

- What type of opportunity would entice you to leave the company?
- What would your boss say if you told him that you wanted his position in three years?

- What do your top competitors do better than your company?
- If you had to work for a competitor, which would you choose and why?
- If there was a rapid downturn in the business, which department or group's headcount would be hit most severely?
- In what areas would your top clients say you need the most improvement?
- What are the biggest potential legal/regulatory/reputational risks your business faces, if any?

Candidate Questions: Personal Growth

- What single piece of information do you know now that you wish you would have known when you started out?
- What responsibilities and skills do you expect successful candidates to acquire after three years in a position?
- Have you had a mentor in your career, and how did she help you? What should I look for in a mentor?

Candidate Questions: Miscellaneous

- In addition to the major industry group, are there any other industry groups I can join to gain a practitioner's perspective while I am still in school?
- How is recruiting coordinated across regions? Is it centralized at headquarters or are decisions exclusively made locally? (This is a good question if you are interested in working overseas.)

- What opportunities have you seen for junior people to work on overseas assignments?

"Do you have any questions about my background or qualifications?" This is a filler question you shouldn't ask. If something were missing, the interviewer would have brought it up earlier. Do not waste the valuable opportunity to ask a more insightful question.

Despite what you may read, there are no "Secret Questions Everyone *Must* Ask to Get the Offer!" Interviewers will react differently to the same questions, so, unfortunately, there is no silver bullet. Judge for yourself which ones make the most sense to you, and ask the questions you believe will make the best impression on the interviewer.

The last part of acing the interview requires the proper follow up to confirm your interest in the position and to demonstrate your professional etiquette.

Actionable Thank You Notes

Thank you letters should be sent out on the day of the interview and be three or four short paragraphs long at most. Email is the preferred format because it will arrive much quicker than a handwritten note.

You want to show that you were paying attention to what the interviewer was saying, so expound upon a relevant point he brought up during the interview. If possible, include a link to a discussion point from the conversation so the interviewer has an action item to follow up on. This can be a professional point you had raised, some useful software or app, a personal point, or some extracurricular activity that may be useful for his kids. Point out a link to an article you wrote if you were on the school newspaper or your blog if you have one, and weave it into your story. It all depends on what was discussed in the interview.

Close by confirming your interest in the position. There's no need to recount all of the reasons you are such a great fit—one or two points are enough.

A company made the effort to call the career services office of a well-known university for the express purpose of informing the career counselor that it will not be extending offers to two of the school's students for summer internships. The company said the candidates were very impressive during their respective interviews, but neither had sent a thank you note. The counselor told me he always tells students to send thank you notes on the day of their interviews; the students just didn't take the advice.

Following proper business protocols is particularly important for students because they have less experience to rely on to support their candidacy. Some people say that thank you letters don't matter much, but there is absolutely no question that some employers do care as the previous anecdote confirmed. There is no harm in sending them, so just spend the two or three minutes it takes to write and send your thank you notes.

How Should You Follow Up and How Often?

Texting is not an appropriate mode of communication when contacting potential employers. Formal business language and practices are important as they reflect your communication skills and professionalism.

A summer intern candidate passed several rounds of interviews at a boutique investment bank. Possibly because of the friendliness exhibited by the manager, the candidate felt comfortable following up on an issue by texting the manager a message that started, "Hey, Hank," The candidate did not receive an offer because the manager felt the candidate was not acting in a professional manner.

The lesson of this anecdote is, "*Do not confuse informality with familiarity.*"

Emails, phone calls, or even handwritten notes are all acceptable ways to follow up after the initial thank you email. Follow the guidance of the interviewer or human resources about how long you should wait to follow up. In the absence of any direction, weekly or bi-weekly follow up is fine. Keep in mind that there is a fine line between aggressively following up to express your interest and annoying someone to the point that it will negatively affect your chance of getting an offer.

Choosing the Right References

I have yet to have any candidate provide me a bad reference, but it is worth the effort to prep your references for each specific position. Use the references who are the most eloquent and who know you best. In keeping with the principle of using every opportunity to differentiate yourself at every step of the recruiting process, even a discussion of references can be differentiating:

When a potential employer asked me for references, I asked him for the top three or four clients the company was targeting but hasn't been able to engage at a senior level. I provided strategic references at several of these target clients and soon received the job offer.

Although this particular strategy is premature for students just starting their career, it is worth mentioning as an example of applying the sales mindset to every aspect of your job search; no detail is too small to make a difference. By figuring out how you can provide immediate value to prospective employers, you will greatly improve your chances of getting the job offer.

Chapter 11
Converting Internships into Full-Time Offers

THE PREVIOUS CHAPTERS explained what is needed to land your internship or job. If this book has helped you land your first job, congratulations! This chapter is for students who have landed internships and want to maximize their experience and chances of turning internships into job offers. You should treat your summer internship as a really long and thorough interview. This doesn't mean you need to be paranoid about everything you do, but, that said, everything you do will reflect on your candidacy.

First, act professionally. This includes completing tasks on time. It is your manager's job to set priorities for the group, so complete the work he assigns to you first before trying to take on other projects. Next, you can demonstrate your value to the group and exhibit the behaviors that managers value and reward with some of the ideas detailed below.

Productivity on Day One

You can actually be productive starting on day one in the office. As mentioned in the "Technical Skills" section, one of the possible expectations of interns and new grads is help with the organization of materials. Here, you can kill two birds with one stone. For example, by helping the team organize its group computer directories, you can quickly see which projects and transactions the group is working on. Throughout my career from associate to managing director, one of the first things I have done when I've joined a new company is scan through the group's directories, and they are often a mess.

Start by looking through the group's directories to see whether they can be better organized. Invariably, the answer will be yes. Ask your manager whether you can help improve the layout of the directories and files. If the manager agrees, do it, and then share the results with the team so everyone will know where to find everything. Be careful that there aren't macros or programs that are reliant on the names of the directories and location of files.

Look for a group calendar or dashboard to find out when important meetings or events are coming up. Also, see whether there is a key account list so you will know when particularly important clients are being discussed, and learn how you can assist.

Review the organizational chart for your group/division so you are aware of the priorities of tasks when requested by people other than your direct manager.

Volunteer for meetings because you will likely learn

things and possibly be assigned interesting work. Take notes and summarize the meeting with action items in an email (have your manager check before sending it out). I have seen associates show up at meetings empty-handed (no notebook). Work is not a spectator sport; you are expected to participate.

When asked to help prepare presentations:

- Graphics convey information much more succinctly than words.
- Less is more with regard to the overall content as well as the amount of information on any one slide (otherwise, the audience will be too busy reading the slides to listen to what the presenter is saying).
- When you draft a new presentation, there should be a "Money Slide"—the single slide you would present if you could only present one, usually about making money, saving money, or taking an action. (If you cannot articulate the crux of the presentation on a single slide, you do not really understand the transaction or ideas.)
- When asked to make edits, create a checklist to ensure all requested changes have been implemented; this attention to detail will help you stand out because it is not unusual for interns to return presentations with incomplete edits.
- Ensure formatting consistency, including using the same bullet point types, indentation spacing, fonts, and graphics throughout the presentation.

When creating spreadsheets:

- Label cells descriptively.
- Add comments to cells.
- Color code input cells.
- Place column totals at the top of the spreadsheet rather than at the bottom.
- Freeze panes to preserve headings, if applicable.

These suggestions make it easier for others to use, maintain, and modify the spreadsheets. Your manager and teammates will appreciate your teamwork and consideration.

When you are using corporate resources such as computers at work, you should have no expectations of privacy. Every email you send, every website you visit, and the amount of time you spend web-surfing can all be monitored by the company. You are using its equipment and you are "on its time" so it has every legal and commercial right to ensure resources are used responsibly and for business purposes.

As an example of how seriously companies treat violations of their computer policies, an employee was terminated at a company because he went on another employee's computer (while the second employee was away from his desk) and sent files to his own personal email account. The reasons for termination were two-fold; firstly, unauthorized use of another employee's computer, and secondly, sending company information to a personal account.

Exhibiting a Sense of Urgency

Respond promptly to emails, phone calls, or any requests or assignments. However, time management is about efficiency and prioritization, not just speed. For example, if important tasks take much longer, but shorter, less important tasks are keeping others from moving ahead with their work, finish the shorter task first. Break down large tasks into smaller ones so you can show small wins and provide the opportunity for feedback to ensure you are on the right track.

There is a caveat; don't try to take on too much work and try to be a hero because that can easily backfire. In an over-eager attempt to impress people, a rookie mistake is to over-promise and under-deliver. In finance, this is called a wrong way trade where there is limited upside with significant downside. If your schedule is slipping, communicate with your boss during the assignment rather than waiting until the very end when you realize you cannot finish on time. Maybe additional resources can be provided or the deadline changed. But at least the boss is aware and can plan accordingly. You might think admitting that you are struggling conveys weakness, but if you wait too long to inform your boss, she won't be able to do anything to rectify the situation, which makes both of you look bad.

Treat your manager's time like a limited commodity, but don't be afraid to ask questions for clarification. It is more important to do the work right the first time than to rush through it with unclear objectives—which could end in incorrect results and create more work for everyone later.

Get up to speed quickly by studying in the evenings, not during business hours. Don't squander the opportunity to interact with colleagues by sticking your nose in a book or in front of a computer during the day, even if it is work-related.

Even if your supervisor has not given you work to do, you should never be idle as an intern. If you've completed all of your assigned tasks, be proactive and offer to help with a specific task. If you can't think of anything specific, ask your supervisor whether there's anything you can do to help. If the answer is no, see whether you can help someone else in the department; he will appreciate it, and it will allow you to make another contact in the company. If you find no one needs your assistance, find a way to make yourself useful. Is there a need for a database or spreadsheet that could collect information in one place and would be useful to the entire team? Could an existing database or template be improved to maximize efficiency? Perhaps there's an application or software package you can introduce to your supervisor that might come in handy for scheduling, conducting meetings, or sharing information. Is there a storage space that could use a little TLC?

Walk quickly because image matters. This concept is related to the previous paragraph about never being idle as an intern. You don't want to appear frenzied, but you do want to project the image that you are focused and determined.

Taking Ownership and Responsibility

The best way to engender trust and loyalty from your manager is by consistently saying, "I'll take care of it." Taking ownership of a task and getting it done efficiently, without drama, is the basis of a productive, low-maintenance employee. You will quickly become your manager's go-to person if your focus is on getting the job done regardless of whose responsibility it is. The late Jimmy Lee, former vice-chairman of JP Morgan Chase, once spoke at one of our team's off-sites and offered a great piece of advice: "I pay my people a lot of money to bring me solutions, not problems."

One of the more annoying habits managers deal with is listening to employees make excuses. One of the more prevalent ones is, "It fell through the cracks." No, things do not just fall through cracks; you just didn't do it. What if payroll called to tell you, "Sorry, your paycheck fell through the cracks this month"? You wouldn't find that acceptable, would you? If you make a mistake, simply admit it, apologize, move on, and make sure it does not become a habit.

Many people do not take constructive criticism well because they mistakenly view it as a personal attack on their skills or work. Treat criticism, especially in regard to minor issues related to your productivity or inter-personal skills, as a learning and self-improvement experience. Cheerfully accept your manager's comments and take the situation a step further by asking for any additional advice to improve your performance. This request will be unexpected and is an additional opportunity to differentiate yourself from others.

Answer the Question

A pet peeve of mine is when people do not answer the questions asked of them before they launch into excuses. If someone asks whether a task assigned to you was completed, the only correct answer is either yes or no; if the person asks why, then obviously it's fine to explain afterwards.

A variation on this is when I ask whether something was completed by someone else. For example, "Was the proposal sent out to the client?" The only correct answers are yes, no, or I'll find out now. "I think so" is not an appropriate answer because this is a factual question, not a request for an opinion. If I relied on the "I think so" answer and the answer was actually no, even though it was my fault for accepting it, your credibility would suffer.

Email Etiquette

Email etiquette is an important topic because the prevalence of texting has created a shortcut language that is inappropriate in many business environments. Not only are negative or derogatory terms unacceptable, but even positive or neutral terms such as "tnx vm", "gr8", "lol", "Idk", "lmk", do not belong in most business correspondences. There may be exceptions at small start-ups, but as an intern, err on the side of caution until you get a better understanding of the company's level of formality.

The value of an email is inversely correlated to the number of its recipients. Everyone will assume someone else on that long list will read it and follow up, and it's possible no one actually will follow up. You may also be perceived as overtly political by being overly self-promotional. Limit the recipients to those people who need the information or need to take action.

There is almost no situation where blind copy (bcc) is appropriate. One of the few valid reasons for using bcc is when the company broadcasts an email to a large audience and it doesn't want to show a distribution list of hundreds or thousands of recipients.

A colleague had sent an email to a group of us and bcc'd our manager. The manager "replied all" to the email. You do not have to be an expert in email forensics to figure out that the sender was not being a team player and had a hidden agenda. This created distrust, which is very difficult to recover from.

Always copy (cc) your manager when sending an email to anyone at your manager's level or higher. Doing this will prevent your manager from being caught off-guard.

Never send an email in anger. Wait a few hours, or even a full day, to give yourself time to calm down and think through the situation rationally. As the saying goes, "*You cannot un-ring the bell.*"

Socialize

Be the first person in the office and the last one out at least a few days a week. These are often the best times to chat with the more senior members of the group since they are likely less harried. You also get the additional benefit of showing your commitment to the opportunity. Use this extra time to learn about the company's products or the industry and not just be in the office for the sake of putting in face-time.

Companies make significant efforts to maximize the internship experience, so you need to take advantage of all opportunities: lunches with management, mentorship programs, cross-disciplinary presentations, training and skills development classes, and extracurricular activities such as sports events and concerts.

Even though you will formally report to a manager in the department, most of your day-to-day tasks will be assigned and evaluated by lower-level employees in the group. Do not underestimate the influence of these employees when it comes to whether you receive a full-time job offer because the manager will rely heavily on their opinions. Your job is to make everyone else's job easier.

Don't be shy about asking for exposure to other areas of the company and people outside of your immediate department, but do some research about the functions rather than just show up and ask, "So, what do you do?" Learn how others interact with your group. People are willing to help out as long as they see you are making an effort and not just asking to be spoon-fed information.

Respecting All

Most interns understand that managing up—being respectful and cognizant of the image you convey to senior members of the organization—is important. They are less likely to know that managers will often form a strong opinion of a person based on how she treats junior or support people. If someone is dismissive or disrespectful to junior or support staff, that person will likely be a poor team player, and nobody wants to work with someone like that.

An associate was berating an administrative assistant in the middle of the office because of a minor mistake she made. He told her, "Our only job is to make our boss look good." I corrected him by saying, "Our job is to make our boss look good by doing great work, not focusing on superficial issues." A secondary issue that will be useful to you later in your career is that if you need to reprimand someone, do it in private.

As the title of this chapter implies, the goal of an internship is to get a full-time job offer. However, what should you do if you discover during the internship that the position is not a good fit? If it is early in the internship, you may have a chance to move to a different area. Otherwise, continue to do the best job you can because the goal is still to receive an offer. After you receive the offer, you can try to negotiate a position in a different department. The offer can also be valuable as you have discussions with other companies because you can use it as leverage to get quicker responses and even additional job offers. The bottom line is that you want to have the option to convert the offer into something that works for you.

Chapter 12
Parting Thoughts

W E HAVE COVERED everything you need to do from the beginning of your first year through to your senior year to land your dream job. If you have made it to this point in the book, you may feel like you have been drinking through a fire-hose. A lot of information and opinions were presented, some of which you may have agreed with and some of which you didn't. And that is perfectly fine because there is no one right way to get a job—what impresses one interviewer may turn off another.

The key principles covered in this book are applicable to all positions and all industries. The most important takeaways are:

- Among a field of other well-qualified candidates, differentiate yourself from the competition with your actions, questions, answers, and motivations.
- It is your job to provide interviewers with the information they need to promote your candidacy.

- Create stories to engage with your interviewers and connect on an emotional level.
- Be specific with your explanations and answers so they are memorable and leave a strong positive impression.
- Develop the mindset and discipline of a good salesperson. Like sales, job hunting is a numbers game where your best chance of success comes from continuously cultivating your network, reaching out to learn about the industry, developing your interview skills, and following up. That does not mean you should aimlessly send out resumes with the hope that something "sticks."

Work on the strategies and techniques you find helpful, even if they are initially outside of your comfort zone. Everyone has to make decisions and take action based on incomplete information—get used to this reality and learn to trust in your efforts and abilities. I will leave you with three quotes that sum this all up:

"Knowledge isn't power…action is power."
— Anthony Robbins, motivational speaker

"The only place success comes before work is in the dictionary."
— Vince Lombardi, former NFL player and coach

"There is no try, only do."
— Yoda, Jedi Master

About the Author

Jerome is a native New Yorker and is a proud product of its public school system. He was particularly fortunate to attend the Bronx High School of Science, which has produced eight Nobel Prize winners, seven in physics and one in chemistry. What has stuck with him from his high school experience is that re-  gardless of your social or economic background, success can be nurtured and developed with the proper guidance and encouragement.

Upon graduating from Tufts University with a B.S. in Electrical Engineering, Jerome started his career in technology. After working for several years in technical positions, Jerome transitioned into a series of sales roles where he found his true calling: being in front of clients and closing deals. Over the past twenty-five years, he has continued to learn about salesmanship and hone his sales strategies. He describes the sales style he has developed as "a soft-sell by showing, not telling" and focusing on both the direct and less obvious requirements of clients to win deals.

After graduating from Columbia Business School, Jerome began his career in finance in the emerging area of credit derivatives at Chemical Bank in 1996. After working several years in New York, he relocated to London for Citibank with his young family. He ran credit structuring groups in Europe, which involved explaining complex products to clients in the simplest terms possible and continuing to develop his sales skills. After three years in London, Jerome moved to Hong Kong to expand UBS's credit structuring business in Asia.

Jerome is fortunate to have lived in and visited vibrant and diverse locales around the world. His daughters had seen Big Ben, the Eiffel Tower, and the Roman Coliseum by the time they had started kindergarten. Jerome climbed the Great Wall of China with his family, jumped off of 2,000 meter cliffs to paraglide in New Zealand, and gained his scuba-diving certification in Phuket. He has come full circle and is now back living in the greater New York City area. His current activities include teaching a graduate-level finance course at the Gabelli School of Business at Fordham University and mentoring startups through his angel network, Angelus Funding.

Throughout his career in the U.S., Europe, and Asia, Jerome was actively recruiting college students for the companies he has worked for. His experience sitting on the other side of the interview table from the candidates, combined with his sales experience, provides him with unique insights into the hiring decision process. It is this experience that led him to write this book, as well as create his company Real World Experts™. He is looking forward to this next chapter of his career, in which he will advise college students on how to land their dream jobs and launch their careers!

For more information about Jerome, visit him at www.InternshipsAndFirstJob.com.

CPSIA information can be obtained
at www.ICGtesting.com
Printed in the USA
LVOW13s1205200817
545694LV00010B/299/P